Florida Social Studies

Who We Are as Americans

Using Maps

Masterfile/Royalty Free

The White House

Brand X Pictures/PunchStock

Colonial People

Blend Images / Alamy

Toy Store

Draw a picture of a toy.

McGraw Hill **Education**

Bothell, WA • Chicago, IL • Columbus, OH • New York, NY

PROGRAM AUTHORS

James A. Banks, Ph.D.
Kerry and Linda Killinger Endowed
    Chair in Diversity Studies and Director,
    Center for Multicultural Education
University of Washington
Seattle, Washington

Kevin P. Colleary, Ed.D.
Curriculum and Teaching Department
Graduate School of Education
Fordham University
New York, New York

Linda Greenow, Ph.D.
Associate Professor and Chair
Department of Geography
State University of New York at New Paltz
New Paltz, New York

Walter C. Parker, Ph.D.
Professor of Social Studies Education,
    Adjunct Professor of Political
    Science
University of Washington
Seattle, Washington

Emily M. Schell, Ed.D.
Visiting Professor, Teacher Education
San Diego State University
San Diego, California

Dinah Zike
Educational Consultant
Dinah-Might Adventures, L.P.
San Antonio, Texas

CONTRIBUTING AUTHORS

James M. Denham, Ph.D.
Professor of History and Director,
    Lawton M. Chiles, Jr., Center for
    Florida History
Florida Southern College
Lakeland, Florida

M.C. Bob Leonard, Ph.D.
Professor, Hillsborough Community
    College
Director, Florida History Internet Center
Ybor City, Florida

Jay McTighe
Educational Author and Consultant
McTighe and Associates Consulting
Columbia, Maryland

Timothy Shanahan, Ph.D.
Professor of Urban Education &
    Director, Center for Literacy
College of Education
University of Illinois at Chicago

ACADEMIC CONSULTANTS

Tom Daccord
Educational Technology Specialist
Co-Director, EdTechTeacher
Boston, Massachusetts

Joe Follman
Service Learning Specialist
Director, Florida Learn & Serve

Cathryn Berger Kaye, M.A.
Service Learning Specialist
Author, *The Complete Guide to Service
    Learning*

Justin Reich
Educational Technology Specialist
Co-Director, EdTechTeacher
Boston, Massachusetts

Mc Graw Hill Education

Copyright © 2013 The McGraw-Hill Companies, Inc.

Send all inquiries to:
McGraw-Hill Education
8787 Orion Place
Columbus, OH 43240

ISBN: 978-0-02-114677-2
MHID: 0-02-114677-2

Printed in the United States of America.

7 8 9 QLM 16 15 14

Common Core State Standards© Copyright 2010. National Governors Association Center
for Best Practices and Council of Chief State School Officers. All rights reserved.

Understanding by Design® is a registered trademark of the
Association for Supervision and Curriculum Development ("ASCD").

The McGraw-Hill Companies

BACK COVER: (top to bottom, left to right) The McGraw-Hill Companies, Getty Images, Joshua Ets-Hokin/Getty Images, Jose Luis Pelaez Inc/Blend Images/CORBIS, Digital Vision/Getty Images.

Explore! UNIT 1 Our World

BIG IDEA Maps help us understand the world.

My Book

My Computer

networks

 Go online and find this interactive thematic map.

My Cover

Find the bird on the cover. In which direction is she flying?

Left

EXplore! UNIT 2 Native Americans

BIG IDEA Culture influences the way people live.

My Book

My Computer

 Go online and find this interactive map of Native American Regions.

My Cover

Find the National Museum of the American Indian on the cover. Draw a picture of something you might see inside this museum.

Keep going! Next we'll explore Colonial America and government!

My Book

My Computer

networks

 Go online and find a video about the Statue of Liberty.

John Wang/Getty Images

My Cover

Find the people dressed in colonial clothing on the cover. Then draw a person dressed in colonial clothing.

Explore! UNIT 4 Citizens and Government

BIG IDEA 💡 People's actions affect others.

My Book

My Computer

networks

 Go online and find this interactive map of Washington, D.C.

My Cover

Find the White House on your cover.

Who lives and works in the White House?

_____

_____

Keep going!
Next we'll explore economics!

Explore! UNIT 5 All About Economics

BIG IDEA Relationships affect choices.

My Computer

networks

 Go online and find this image of businesses in a community.

My Cover

Find the service workers and places that provide goods on the cover.

List two service workers.

_____ _____

List two goods that are sold in shops.

_____

Explore! Skills and Maps

1 Our World

 BIG IDEA **Maps help us understand the world.**

Have you ever used a map? In this unit, you will learn all about maps. You will learn about different kinds of maps and how to use them. You will also find out how maps help us to understand the world better.

NGSS Standards SS.2.G.1.3: Label on a map or globe the continents, oceans, Equator, Prime Meridian, North and South Pole. **SS.2.G.1.4:** Use a map to locate the countries in North America (Canada, United States, Mexico, and the Caribbean Islands).

networks

There's More Online!
● Skill Builders
● Vocabulary Flashcards

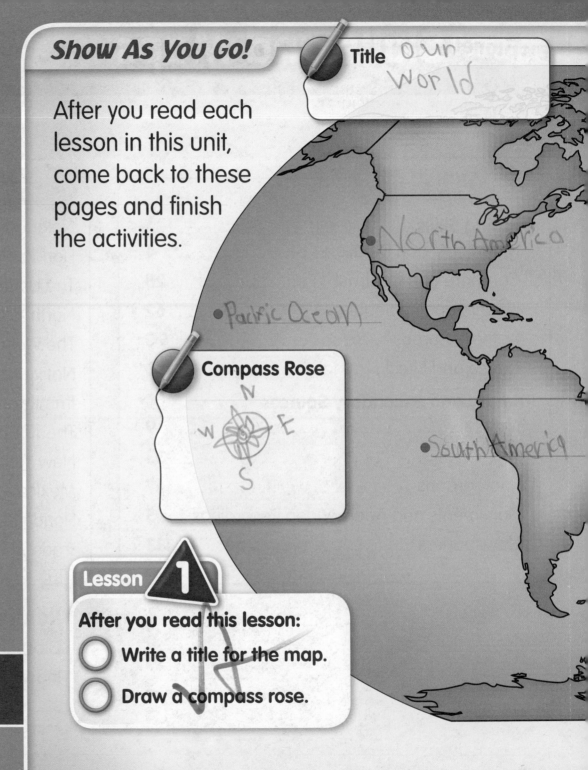

Show As You Go!

After you read each lesson in this unit, come back to these pages and finish the activities.

Title Our World

•North America

•Pacific Ocean

Compass Rose

•South America

Lesson 1

After you read this lesson:

○ Write a title for the map.

○ Draw a compass rose.

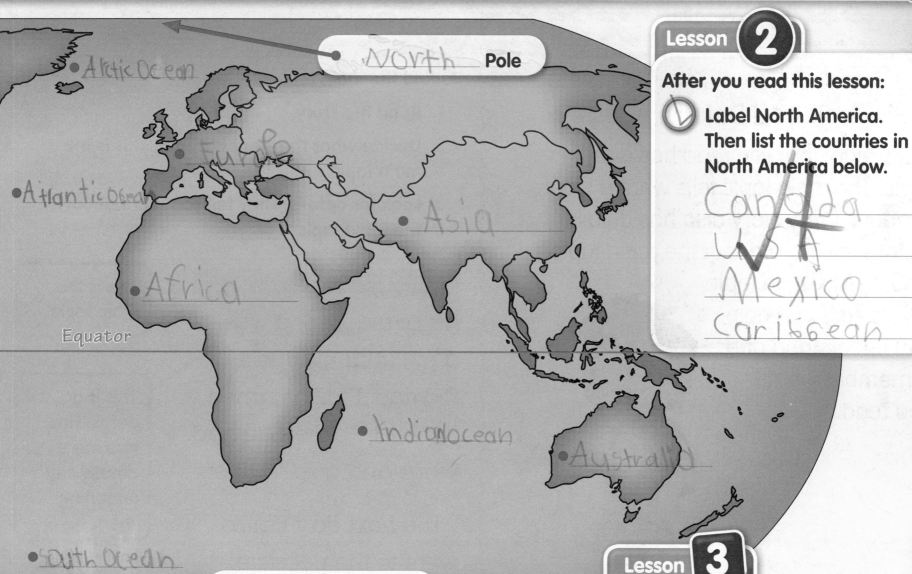

North **Pole**

Arctic Ocean

Europe

Atlantic ocean

Asia

Africa

Equator

Indian ocean

Australia

South Ocean

south **Pole**

Antarctica

Fold page here

Lesson 2

After you read this lesson:

Label North America. Then list the countries in North America below.

Canada

USA

Mexico

Caribbean

Lesson 3

After you read this lesson:

Label the continents, oceans, and North and South Pole.

3

Common Core Standards

RI.2: Identify the main topic of a multiparagraph text as well as the focus of specific paragraphs within the text.

Main Topic and Details

Every story that you read has a main topic. The main topic tells what a story is about. Every story also has details. Details tell more about the main topic. Finding the main topic and details can help you understand and remember what you read.

 **Learn It**

To find the main topic and details:

1. **Read the story.**

2. **Decide what the story is about. This is the main topic.**

3. **Look for details. They tell you more about the main topic.**

Emilio got a pet bird for his birthday. She was a gift from his Uncle Ricardo. Emilio named the bird Goldie. She had white and gold feathers.

> **This is the main topic.**

> **This is a detail. Find two more details and underline them.**

The next day Emilio went to the pet store. He bought a cage for Goldie. He also bought her some food.

Write the main topic and details from the story on page 4 in the chart below.

Main Topic

Emillio got a pet bird for his birthday.

Detail

a gift
named it Goldie
White and gold
feathehers

Detail

Bought a
cage
bought food

Read the story below. Circle the main topic. Underline the details in each paragraph.

One day Goldie flew away. She flew out an open window. Emilio called his friend Lily to help him look for her.

First Emilio and Lily looked for her in the yard. They saw her fly away from Emilio's house. So, they followed her.

Words to Know

Common Core Standard
RI.4: Determine the meaning of words and phrases in a text relevant to a grade 2 topic or subject area.

The list below shows some important words you will learn in this unit. Their definitions can be found on the next page. Read the words.

thematic map p. 12

political map p. 14

physical map p. 18

globe p. 22

FOLDABLES®

The Foldable on the next page will help you learn these important words. Follow the steps below to make your Foldable.

Step 1  Cut along the dotted blue lines.

Step 2  Fold along the dotted orange lines.

Step 3 Trace the words and read their definitions.

Step 4 Complete the activities.

This thematic map shows Florida's

_____ .

A. zoos

B. airports

C. parks

This is a political map of the United States. Color the state of Florida.

A **thematic map** tells us certain information about a place.

A **political map** shows the borders of states, countries, and other areas.

A **physical map** shows different land and water features, such as lakes, mountains, and rivers.

A **globe** is a round model of the Earth.

This physical map shows lakes and rivers in Florida. Trace the lakes and rivers.

Draw a globe.

physical map

globe

Fold Here

thematic map

political map

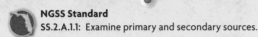
Primary Sources

NGSS Standard
SS.2.A.1.1: Examine primary and secondary sources.

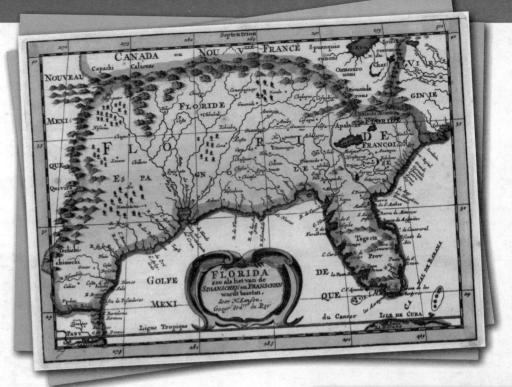

Learn about Florida through primary sources! Primary sources are written or made by someone who saw an event happen. They teach us about people, places, and events.

Maps are one type of primary source. A map is a drawing of what a place looks like from above. We can learn about what people thought places looked like long ago by studying old maps. This map of Florida was created in 1662. That is more than 300 years ago!

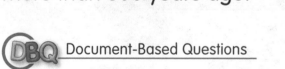 Document-Based Questions

University of Alabama Historical Map Archive/Courtesy of Whitney Telle, Northport, Alabama

netw⊚rks
There's More Online!
● Skill Builders
● Resource Library

Look at the map on this page. What does it show?

Florida in 1662

How is this map different from a map of Florida today?

it show Florida much Bigger!

Using Maps

 Essential Question

Why are maps important?
What do you think?

Maps help us find our way.

Word Hunt

Find and circle these words:

thematic map   map scale

compass rose   map key

*element

intermediate directions

NGSS Standards SS.2.G.1.1: Use different types of maps (political, physical, and thematic) to identify map elements.

Maps

One morning Emilio noticed that his pet bird, Goldie, was missing. "Oh no!" he told his friend Lily. "We have to find Goldie! I think I saw her fly toward the park."

Which item should Emilio and Lily use to get to the park?
Circle your answer.

Emilio and Lily got a map of their neighborhood to help them find the park. A map is a drawing that shows where places are located. A neighborhood map will show Emilio and Lily how to get to the park.

What is a map?

A drawing that shows where places are.

NGSS Standards SS.2.G.1.1: Use different types of maps (political, physical, and thematic) to identify map elements.

Reading Skill

Ask and Answer Questions One thing you should do when you read something is to ask and answer questions about the text.

1. Who is this story about? Circle their names in the text.

2. What is the problem in the story?

Emilio's bird is missing.

Map Elements

"How will we read the map?" asked Lily. Emilio told her that maps have different **elements**, or parts. "The map elements will help us read the map," he said. Emilio explained each element to Lily.

Emilio and Lily used the map to find the park. When they got there, they looked for Goldie.

A **map scale** shows how far apart places really are on a map. On this scale, one inch equals ten yards.

Neighborhood Map

This is a **thematic map** of a neighborhood. A thematic map tells us certain information about a place or area.

The title of a map tells what area is shown.

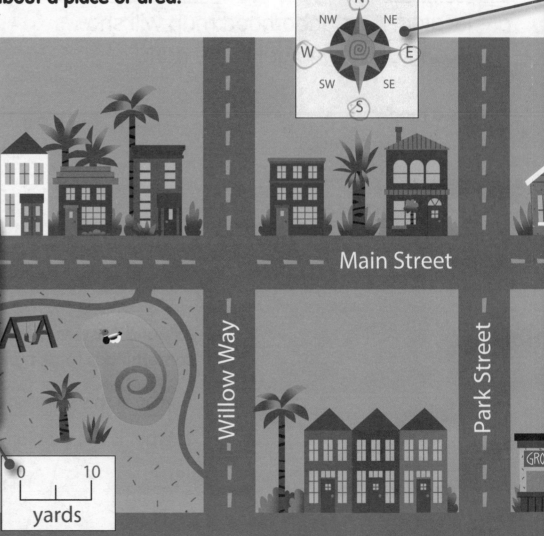

N
NW   NE
W   E
SW   SE
S

Main Street

Willow Way

Park Street

0   10
yards

GRO

A **compass rose** shows the cardinal directions—north, south, east, and west. It also shows the intermediate directions—northeast, northwest, southeast, and southwest.

A **map key**, or **map legend**, tells what the pictures on a map mean.

Emilio and Lily just saw Goldie fly away from the park! They think she might have flown toward Tallahassee, Florida.

MAP KEY

 library

 park

 grocery store

 school

1. Draw a school in the map key.

2. Color the map scale red.

3. In what direction is the library from the beach?

NW

LIBRARY

Beach Street

FIRE STATION

Lesson 1

? **Essential Question** Why are maps important?

They help us know where we are going.

Go back to *Show As You Go!* on pages 2–3.

NGSS Standards SS.2.G.1.1: Use different types of maps (political, physical, and thematic) to identify map elements.

netw✦rks **There's More Online!** ● Games ● Assessment

Where We Live

NGSS Standards SS.2.G.1.1: Use different types of maps. (political, physical, and thematic) to identify map elements. **SS.2.G.1.2:** Using maps and globes, locate the student's hometown, Florida, and North America, and locate the state capital and the national capital.

? Essential Question

How do maps help us find places?

What do you think?

_____

_____

_____

 Word Hunt

Find and (circle) these words:

political map   physical map

*travel

Find 2 more new words:

_____

_____

Florida

Emilio and Lily live in Miami, Florida. They used a map of Florida to help them get to Tallahassee. When Emilio and Lily got there, they looked all over the city for Goldie.

This is a **political map**. A political map shows the borders of states, countries, and other areas. On this map, the capital city, Tallahassee, is marked with a star. Other cities are marked with dots.

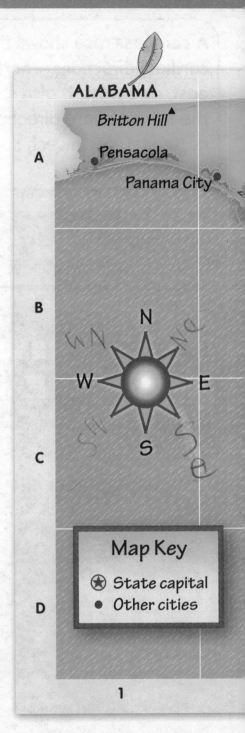

ALABAMA

Britton Hill

Pensacola

Panama City

A

B

C

D

N
W   E
S

Map Key

⊛ State capital
● Other cities

1

Florida: Political

GEORGIA

★ Tallahassee

Suwannee River

Gainesville

Jacksonville

St. Johns River

Lake George

FLORIDA

Orlando

Kissimmee

Daytona Beach

Cape Canaveral

Gulf of Mexico

Tampa

Lake Kissimmee

Kissimmee River

St. Petersburg

Tampa Bay

Sarasota

Lake Okeechobee

Fort Myers

THE EVERGLADES

Port St. Lucie

West Palm Beach

Ft. Lauderdale

Miami

ATLANTIC OCEAN

| 0 | 50 | 100 miles |

| 0 | 50 | 100 kilometers |

Key West

FLORIDA KEYS

3   4   5

Emilio and Lily saw Goldie fly away from Tallahassee!

1. **Draw yourself in the city closest to your hometown.**

2. **Fill in the intermediate directions on the compass rose.**

3. **Circle the capital of Florida on the map.**

The boxes on this map are part of a coordinate grid. The coordinate grid helps to break the map up into smaller sections.

15

The United States

Emilio and Lily think Goldie flew north. "We need a map of the United States," Lily said. "It will help us **travel** north."

"Maybe she flew to our nation's capital, Washington, D.C.," Emilio said.

Emilio and Lily used a map of the United States to get to Washington, D.C. Once there, they looked all over for Goldie.

Washington, D.C.

The United States: Political

ALASKA

0   200   400 miles

0   200 400 kilometers

WASHINGTON

OREGON

IDAHO

MONTANA

WYOMING

NORTH DAKOTA

SOUTH DAKOTA

NEBRASKA

NEVADA

UTAH

COLORADO

KANSAS

CALIFORNIA

ARIZONA

NEW MEXICO

OKL

TEXAS

HAWAII

0   100   200 miles

0   100 200 kilometers

NGSS Standards **SS.2.G.1.1:** Use different types of maps. (political, physical, and thematic) to identify map elements. **SS.2.G.1.2:** Using maps and globes, locate the student's hometown, Florida, and North America, and locate the state capital and the national capital.

Glowimages / Alamy Images

MINNESOTA
VERMONT MAINE
WISCONSIN
NEW HAMPSHIRE
MICHIGAN
NEW YORK
MASSACHUSETTS
RHODE ISLAND
CONNECTICUT
IOWA
PENNSYLVANIA
NEW JERSEY
ILLINOIS
OHIO
DELAWARE
INDIANA
WEST VIRGINIA
Washington, D.C.
MISSOURI
MARYLAND
VIRGINIA
KENTUCKY
NORTH CAROLINA
ARKANSAS
TENNESSEE
SOUTH CAROLINA
MISSISSIPPI
GEORGIA
ALABAMA
⊛Tallahassee
LOUISIANA
FLORIDA

NW N NE
W   E
SW S SE

0   200   400 miles
0   200   400 kilometers

Emilio and Lily saw Goldie fly away from Washington, D.C.!

1. Find your state on the map and circle it.

2. Draw a box around Washington, D.C.

North America

Emilio and Lily think Goldie flew north towards Canada.

"How will we find our way to Canada?" asked Lily.

"We can use a map of North America," Emilio explained. "It shows Canada, the United States, Mexico, and the Caribbean Islands."

Emilio and Lily used the map of North America to get to Canada. Once there, they searched everywhere for Goldie.

This is a physical map. A physical map shows different land and water features, such as mountains, rivers, lakes, and oceans.

NGSS Standards SS.2.G.1.1: Use different types of maps. (political, physical, and thematic) to identify map elements. **SS.2.G.1.4:** Use a map to locate the countries in North America (Canada, United States, Mexico, and the Caribbean Islands).

Map Key

Mountains

Rivers

Lakes

River

Mountains

Lake

Emilio and Lily saw Goldie heading east!

1. Draw the symbols in the map key.

2. Locate the countries on the map. Draw:

~~~~~ on Canada

★ on the United States

⋏⋏⋏ on Mexico

● on the Caribbean Islands

Lesson 2

? Essential Question How do maps help us find places?

_____

_____

Go back to *Show As You Go!* on pages 2–3.

networks There's More Online!
◉ Games ◉ Assessment

19

Our Earth

? **Essential Question**

How do we find places on Earth?

What do you think?

_____

_____

_____

_____

Word Hunt

Find and (circle) these words:

Equator   *imaginary

globe   North Pole

South Pole   Prime Meridian

NGSS Standards **SS.2.G.1.1:** Use different types of maps. (political, physical, and thematic) to identify map elements. **SS.2.G.1.2:** Using maps and globes, locate the student's hometown, Florida, and North America, and locate the state capital and the national capital. **SS.2.G.1.3:** Label on a map or globe the continents, oceans, Equator, Prime Meridian, North and South Pole.

The World

Goldie flew away from Canada and headed east over the Atlantic Ocean. Emilio and Lily followed her. They used a map of the world to find their way. A map of the world shows the seven continents and five oceans. Can you see the continents and oceans on this map?

The World

North America

Atlantic Ocean

Pacific Ocean

Equator

South America

This dotted line is the Equator. The Equator is an *imaginary line that runs east and west around the middle of Earth.

This dashed line is the **Prime Meridian**. The Prime Meridian is an imaginary line that runs north and south on Earth.

Emilio and Lily just spotted Goldie! She took off to fly around the world!

1. Connect the dashed line to draw the Prime Meridian.

2. Connect the dots to draw the Equator.

3. What type of map is this?

Political

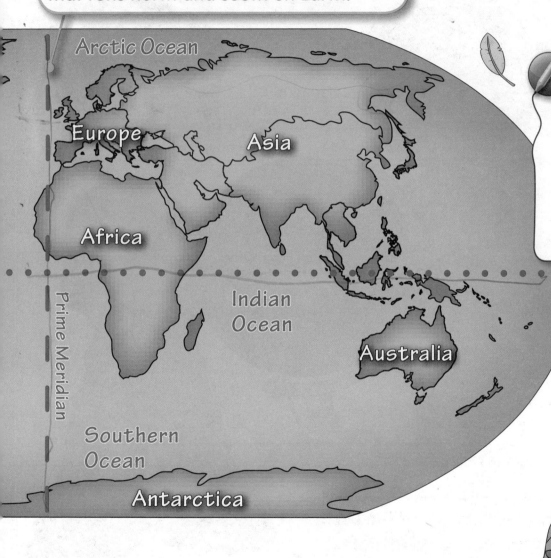

Arctic Ocean

Europe

Asia

Africa

Prime Meridian

Indian Ocean

Australia

Southern Ocean

Antarctica

21

Globes

Emilio and Lily then used a **globe** to see where Goldie might have flown. A globe is a round model of the Earth. You can spin a globe to see each part of Earth.

1. Draw lines for the Equator and Prime Meridian on the globe.

2. Why would you use a globe instead of a map?

You can see the Whole World

NGSS Standards **SS.2.G.1.3:** Label on a map or globe the continents, oceans, Equator, Prime Meridian, North and South Pole.

The very top of the Earth is called the **North Pole**.

The very bottom of the Earth is called the **South Pole**.

Emilio and Lily finally found Goldie on the continent of Asia. They were so happy to find her! They used all of their maps to help them get back home. When they got there, they thought about how maps helped them find places on Earth and bring Goldie back home!

Know and Use text Features Certain text features can help you locate information quickly.

What text features on these pages help you find key words quickly?

Bold print

Highlighting

Lesson **3**

? **Essential Question** How do we find places on Earth?

Go back to *Show As You Go!* on pages 2–3.

 **networks** There's More Online!
● Games ● Assessment

23

Label each picture with a word that descibes it best from the Word Bank.

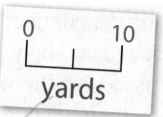

Word Bank

compass rose
map key
map scale
political map
physical map
thematic map

map key

24

Big Idea Project

Now that you have learned about globes, you will make your own! Your teacher will help you make your globe. Make sure to include the items listed below.

As you work, check off each task as you complete it.

My globe...   **Yes it does!**

1. has the continents and oceans labeled.   ○

2. has the Equator and Prime Meridian labeled. ○

3. has the North and South Pole labeled.   ○

4. is colorful and detailed.   ○

Think About the Big Idea

BIG IDEA How do maps help us understand the world? Explain the Big Idea in your own words on the lines below.

_____

_____

_____

BIG IDEA Culture influences the way people live.

Native Americans were the first people to live in North America. Most Native American tribes who lived in the same area shared some elements of their cultures. In this unit, you will learn about the cultures of many Native American tribes.

netw⊙rks

connected.mcgraw-hill.com
○ Skill Builders
○ Vocabulary Flashcards

Show As You Go!

After you read each lesson in this unit, come back to these pages. List what you are learning about the Native Americans of each region.

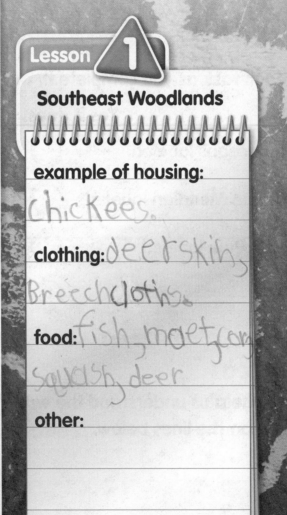

Lesson 1

Southeast Woodlands

example of housing: chickees.

clothing: deerskin, Breechcloths.

food: fish, meat, corn, squash, deer

other:

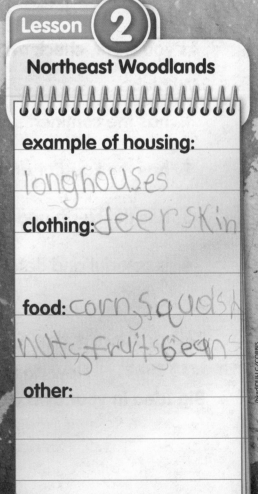

Lesson 2

Northeast Woodlands

example of housing: longhouses

clothing: deerskin

food: corn, squash, nuts, fruits, beans

other:

(bkgd)DULLC/CORBIS

Lesson 3

Plains

example of housing:

Teepes

clothing: Bfloeskin

food: Stew, Buffoo meat, vegetables

other:

Lesson 4

Southwest

example of housing:

clothing:

food:

other:

Lesson 5

Pacific Northwest

example of housing:

clothing:

food:

other:

Lesson 6

After you read this lesson, answer the following question:
How did immigrants impact the lives of Native Americans?

Immigrants forced the N.A. from their land; they brought diseases.

Common Core Standards

R.I.9: Compare and contrast the most important points presented by two texts on the same topic.

Compare and Contrast

Things can be the same or different. We compare things to find out how they are the same. We contrast things to find out how they are different. Comparing and contrasting will help you understand what you read in social studies.

Learn It

To compare and contrast:

1. **Read the story about Scott and Nick.**

2. **Compare Scott and Nick by finding details that are the same.**

3. **Contrast Scott and Nick by finding details that are different.**

Scott and Nick are pen pals. Both boys are in the second grade. Scott lives in Florida. He lives in a highrise apartment by the ocean.

Details that are the same.

Nick lives with his family on a farm in Nebraska. Nick can see barns and fields of corn from his house.

Details that are different.

Compare and contrast the story on page 28 in the chart below. Write the details that are the same in the middle. Write the details that are different in the outer part of each circle.

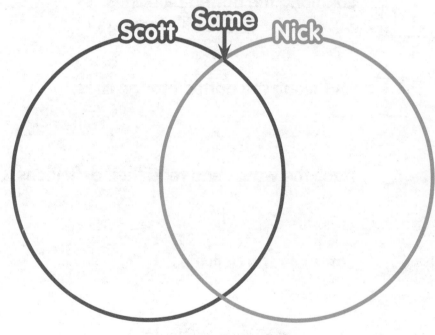

Scott   Same   Nick

Read the story below. Circle details that are the same. Underline the details that are different.

Scott and Nick are very busy boys. Both of them go to school in the morning. Scott walks to school. Nick takes the bus. After school, both boys go to soccer practice. Scott likes to kick the ball. Nick likes to run. On the weekends, Scott and Nick enjoy their free time. Scott likes to swim. Nick likes to go horseback riding.

Words to Know

Common Core Standard
R.I.4: Determine the meaning of words and phrases in a text relevant to a *grade 2 topic* or subject area.

The list below shows some important words you will learn in this unit. Their definitions can be found on the next page.
Read the words.

region p. 34

culture p. 34

prairie p. 43

desert p. 47

immigrant p. 54

settlement p. 54

The Foldable on the next page will help you learn these important words. Follow the steps below to make your Foldable.

Step 1  Cut along the dotted blue lines.

Step 2  Fold along the dotted orange lines.

Step 3 Trace the words and read their definitions.

Step 4 Complete the activities.

(l)Edmond Van Hoorick/Getty Images, (r)Robert Glusic/CORBIS

What kinds of land and water are in the region where you live?

_____

_____

A **region** is an area with common features that make it different from other areas.

Draw a picture of a prairie.

A **prairie** is an area of flat land or rolling hills covered in grasses.

Circle the desert.

A **desert** is a large area of very dry land.

Culture is the beliefs and way of life of a group of people.

An **immigrant** is a person who comes from one country to live in another.

A **settlement** is a place that is newly set up as home.

Write a sentence about what your family's culture is like.

_____

Write a sentence about immigrants moving to the United States.

_____

Draw more houses in this settlement.

culture

immigrant

settlement

region

prairie

desert

Primary Sources

NGSS Standards SS.2.A.1.1: Examine primary and secondary sources.

Artifacts are a type of primary source. An artifact is something that was made or used by people in the past. Artifacts can be things like pots, utensils, or art. You can study artifacts to learn about how people lived long ago.

In this unit, you will learn about different Native American tribes that lived in the United States. The artifacts on this page were used by Native Americans in Florida.

 Document-Based Questions

1. **Look at the image on the right. What are these artifacts made out of?**

   _____

2. **How do you think these artifacts were used?**

   _____

networks
There's More Online!
- Skill Builders
- Resource Library

Native Americans of the Southeast Woodlands

(t)Jack Hollingsworth/CORBIS, (b)Iconotec/Alamy Images

(?) Essential Question

How does where you live affect how you live?

What do you think?

_____

_____

_____

_____

Word Hunt

Find and (circle) these words:

region   culture

*belief

NGSS Standards SS.2.A.2.1: Recognize that Native Americans were the first inhabitants in North America.

The Southeast Woodlands

Hi! My name is Scott. My class has been learning about Native Americans. Native Americans were the first people to live in North America. Native American tribes, or groups, lived in different **regions** of the United States. A region is an area with common features that makes it different from other areas. Look at the map to see all of the regions.

Today our class went on a field trip to the history museum to learn more about Native Americans! Our guide told us that tribes who lived in the same region shared the same **culture**. Culture is the **beliefs** and way of life of a group of people.

Our tour started in a room that showed the daily life of Native Americans in the Southeast Woodlands. The Seminole, Cherokee, and Creek are all tribes that lived in this region.

The Southeast Woodlands was full of trees, plants, and animals. The northern part of the region had mountains and rivers. The southern part had grasses and swamps. Both parts of the region were usually warm and had rain.

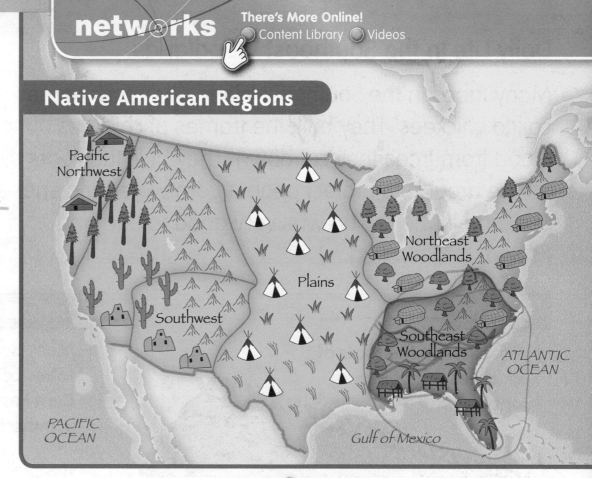

Native American Regions

Pacific Northwest

Southwest

Plains

Northeast Woodlands

Southeast Woodlands

ATLANTIC OCEAN

PACIFIC OCEAN

Gulf of Mexico

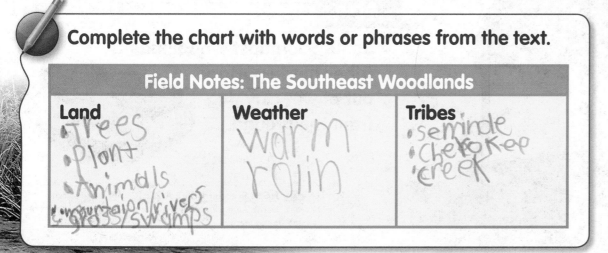

Complete the chart with words or phrases from the text.

Field Notes: The Southeast Woodlands		
Land	**Weather**	**Tribes**
•Trees •Plant •Animals •mountain/rivers •grass/swamps	warm rain	•seminole •cherokee •creek

Map and Globe Skills

Circle the Southeast Woodlands region on the map above.

Daily Life in the Southeast Woodlands

Many tribes in the Southeast Woodlands built homes called chickees. They built the frames of chickees out of wood from trees they cut down. They built the floors up off the ground to protect people from water and snakes. The land in the region was very good for farming, fishing, and hunting.

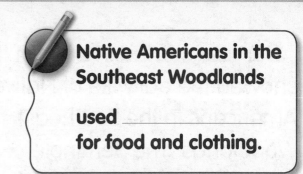

Native Americans in the Southeast Woodlands used _____ **for food and clothing.**

Housing

People built the roofs of chickees out of leaves or grass.

Practices and Beliefs

Many Southeast Woodlands tribes celebrated the Green Corn Festival to honor the summer's first corn crop.

Art

Some Southeast Woodlands tribes made pottery out of wet clay dug from the ground.

NGSS Standard SS.2.A.2.2: Compare the cultures of Native American tribes from various geographic regions of the United States.

(t)Photolink/Getty Images, (b)Getty Images

Clothing

People used deer skin to make their clothing. Men wore breechcloths. Breechcloths are pieces of soft leather. Women wore leather dresses.

Food

Men hunted deer and fished for food. Women dried some of the meat for winter. Women also grew corn and squash.

Lesson 1

? Essential Question How does where you live affect how you live?

_____

_____

_____

Go back to *Show As You Go!* on pages 26–27.

net works

There's More Online!
● Games ● Assessment

Native Americans of the Northeast Woodlands

Essential Question

How did the land in the Northeast Woodlands affect the lives of Native Americans?

What do you think?

_____

_____

_____

Word Hunt

Find and (circle) these words:

crop   *gather

Find two new words.

_____

_____

NGSS Standards SS.2.A.2.2: Compare the
cultures of Native American tribes from various
geographic regions of the United States.

The Northeast Woodlands

Hey! It's Scott again! Next, our tour guide took us into a room that showed us what life was like for Native Americans in the Northeast Woodlands. Did you know the Powhatan and Iroquois are two tribes that lived in the Northeast Woodlands?

Creatas/PunchStock

My class was curious to find out how the land in the Northeast Woodlands was different from the land in the Southeast Woodlands. The guide told us that the Northeast Woodlands was covered in very thick forests. The region was full of rivers, streams, and lakes. There were also many plants and animals. The summers were hot and humid. The winters were cold and snowy. There was a lot of rain, so plants grew well.

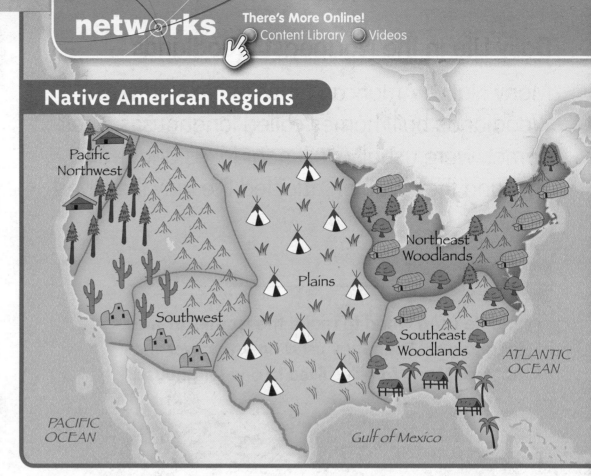

Native American Regions

Pacific Northwest

Southwest

Plains

Northeast Woodlands

Southeast Woodlands

ATLANTIC OCEAN

PACIFIC OCEAN

Gulf of Mexico

Complete the chart with words or phrases from the text.

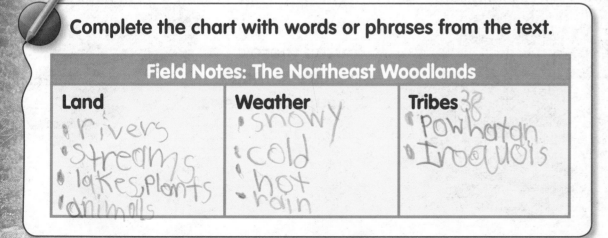

Field Notes: The Northeast Woodlands		
Land	**Weather**	**Tribes**
• rivers	• snowy	• Powhatan
• streams	• cold	• Iroquois
• lakes, plants	• hot	
• animals	• rain	

How does the land in the Northeast Woodlands compare to the land in the Southeast Woodlands?

The land, food, weather, clothings.

39

Daily Life in the Northeast Woodlands

Many Native American tribes in the Northeast Woodlands built homes called longhouses. Their homes were usually built near lakes and rivers. The land they lived on affected the way they lived.

Art

Some tribes would string together beads made out of shells. These shell beads were called wampum. People used wampum as belts or jewelry.

Housing

People used wood to make the frames of their longhouses. Then they used bark to cover the houses. Many families lived in one longhouse.

Food

The most important crops were corn, squash, and beans. People used these crops to make soups and stews.

The men in the Northeast Woodlands fished along the rivers. They also hunted. The land in the region was good for farming. Each spring women planted **crops**. Crops are plants people grow for food or other uses. The women also **gathered** fruits and nuts.

Clothing

Men wore breechcloths in the summer. Women wore dresses. In the winter, they both wore leggings and robes made from animal furs. Both men and women wore shoes called moccasins. These shoes were made from deerskin.

Reading Skill

Compare and Contrast Compare and contrast the cultures of the tribes of the Northeast Woodlands and the Southeast Woodlands.

1. Circle parts of culture that were the same.

2. Underline the parts that were different.

NGSS Standards SS.2.A.2.2: Compare the cultures of Native American tribes from various geographic regions of the United States.

Lesson 2

? Essential Question How did the land in the Northeast Woodlands affect the lives of Native Americans?

The land was good for farming

Go back to *Show As You Go!* on pages 26–27.

There's More Online!
● Games ● Assessment

41

Native Americans of the Plains

? **Essential Question**

How did the land shape the culture of Native Americans on the Plains?

What do you think?

_____

_____

_____

Word Hunt

Find and (circle) these words:

prairie   *herd

Find two new words.

_____

_____

NGSS Standards SS.2.A.2.2: Compare the cultures of Native American tribes from various geographic regions of the United States.

The Plains

Our class has learned a lot about Native Americans of the Southeast and Northeast Woodlands. Next we moved into a room that showed what life was like in the Plains region. The Lakota is one example of a tribe that lived in this region.

Our guide told us that the Plains region was made up of grasslands, valleys, streams, and hills. There were very few trees.

Edmond Van Hoorick/Getty Images

Most of the land in the Plains region was **prairie**. A prairie is an area of flat land or rolling hills covered in grasses. The summers were hot. The winters were long and cold. The Plains got very little rain over the course of a year.

Write a sentence comparing the land in the Northeast Woodlands to the land in the Plains.

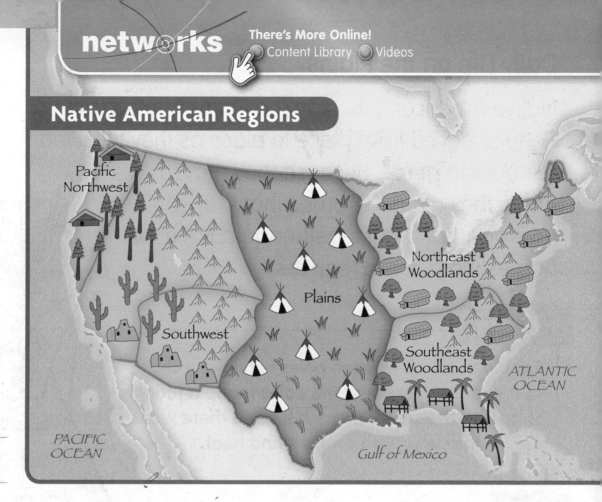

Native American Regions

Pacific Northwest

Southwest

Plains

Northeast Woodlands

Southeast Woodlands

ATLANTIC OCEAN

PACIFIC OCEAN

Gulf of Mexico

Complete the chart with words or phrases from the text.

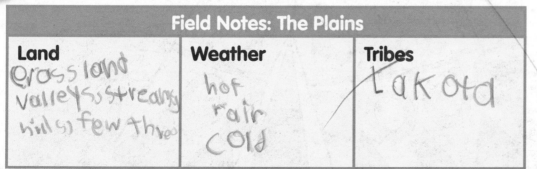

Field Notes: The Plains		
Land	**Weather**	**Tribes**
grass land valleys streams hills few three	hot rair cold	Lakota

Map and Globe Skills

Circle the Plains region on the map.

43

Daily Life on the Plains

Native American tribes on the Plains hunted buffalo. People moved from place to place as they followed the buffalo **herds**. Because they moved so often, they needed homes that they could take apart and put together quickly. These homes were called teepees.

NGSS Standards SS.2.A.2.2: Compare the cultures of Native American tribes from various geographic regions of the United States.

Music

People played music on drums and other instruments. Their music told stories about each tribe.

Housing

People used tall wooden poles set up in a circle to make their teepees. The poles made a triangle shape. In the center of each teepee there was a fire pit that was used for light and heat.

Food

A stew made from buffalo meat and vegetables was a favorite meal.

DLILLC/CORBIS

44

Native Americans on the Plains did not let any part of the buffalo go to waste. When they killed a buffalo, they ate as much of the meat as they could. They dried the rest of the meat so it could be eaten at a later time. People also used the buffalo skins to make clothes, bedding, and covers for their teepees.

Clothing

People made clothing and moccasins out of buffalo skins.

Jules Frazier/Photodisc/Getty Images

Reading Skill

Compare and Contrast Compare and contrast the cultures of the tribes on the Plains and the Northeast Woodlands.

1. Circle parts of culture that were the same.

2. Underline the parts that were different.

Daily Chores

Women stretched and cleaned the buffalo skins. Then they left the skins in the sun to dry.

Lesson 3

? **Essential Question** How did the land shape the culture of Native Americans on the Plains?

_____

_____

_____

Go back to *Show As You Go!* on pages 26–27.

network There's More Online!
● Games ● Assessment

Native Americans of the Southwest

Essential Question

How did the desert affect the lives of Native Americans?

What do you think?

_____

_____

_____

Word Hunt

Find and (circle) these words:

desert   *level

Find two new words.

_____

_____

NGSS Standards SS.2.A.2.2: Compare the cultures of Native American tribes from various geographic regions of the United States.

The Southwest Region

Isn't it interesting how the land shaped Native Americans' ways of life? My class wondered what the land was like in the Southwest region. Many Native American tribes lived in the Southwest. The Pueblo and Navajo are two tribes that lived in this region.

(bkgd)Jeremy Woodhouse/Getty Images

Our guide told us that a lot of the Southwest was **desert**. A desert is a large area of very dry land. The days were very hot, and the nights were cold. Very little rain fell.

(c)Robert Glusic/CORBIS

Native American Regions

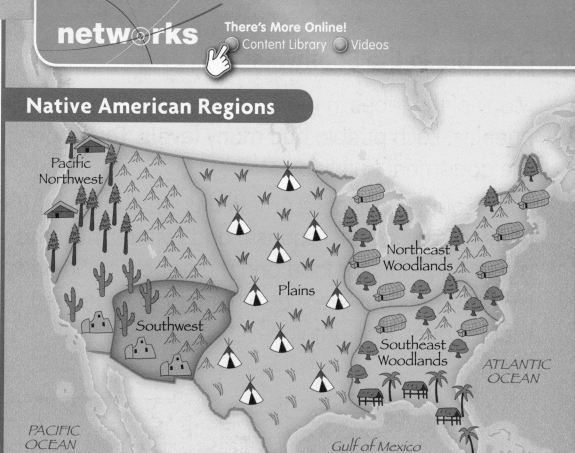

Pacific Northwest

Southwest

Plains

Northeast Woodlands

Southeast Woodlands

PACIFIC OCEAN

ATLANTIC OCEAN

Gulf of Mexico

Complete the chart with words or phrases from the text.

Field Notes: The Southwest		
Land	Weather	Tribes
	Hot cold little rain	

How does the land in the Southwest compare to the land on the Plains?

47

Daily Life in the Southwest

Many of the tribes in the Southwest built homes called pueblos. Each pueblo had many **levels**. They looked like apartment buildings.

The Southwest Native Americans were farmers. They planted corn, beans, squash, and cotton. They also gathered plants for food and medicine. The Southwest Native Americans were also hunters. They hunted rabbits, deer, and antelope.

48

Clothing

Men wore light clothing and sandals in the summer. Women wore cotton dresses. In the winter they both wore leggings and robes. Both men and women wore sandals made from yucca plants.

Art

Some Southwest tribes were known for their fine turquoise jewelry. Turquoise is a blue stone.

digitalfarmer / Alamy

Lesson 4

? Essential Question How did the desert affect the lives of Native Americans?

_____

_____

_____

Go back to *Show As You GO!* on pages 26–27.

 **networks** There's More Online!
  ● Games ● Assessment

Native Americans of the Pacific Northwest

Essential Question

How did the natural resources in the Pacific Northwest affect Native Americans?

What do you think?

Word Hunt

Find and circle this word:

natural resource   *material

Find two new words.

Natural resource are material found in Nature.

NGSS Standards SS.2.A.2.2: Compare the cultures of Native American tribes from various geographic regions of the United States.

The Pacific Northwest

My class had already learned a lot about how Native American tribes of the United States were the same and different. We had just one more region to learn about—the Pacific Northwest. The Tlingit and Kwakiutl are examples of tribes who lived in this region.

Royalty-Free/CORBIS

My class wondered what the land was like in the Pacific Northwest. The guide told us that this land had many trees and plants. There was plenty of food and **natural resources** in the ocean, rivers, and rain forests. Natural resources are **materials** found in nature that people use. The summers were cool, and the winters were mild and wet.

Native American Regions

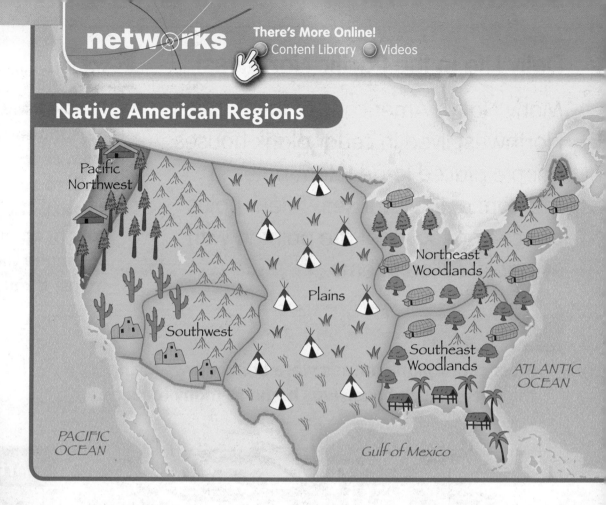

Pacific Northwest

Northeast Woodlands

Plains

Southwest

Southeast Woodlands

ATLANTIC OCEAN

PACIFIC OCEAN

Gulf of Mexico

Complete the chart with words or phrases from the text.

Field Notes: The Pacific Northwest		
Land	**Weather**	**Tribes**
Trees and plants Oceans rivers rainforists	cool summers mild wet winters	Tlingit Kwakiutl

How does the land in the Pacific Northwest compare to the land in the Southwest?

Daily Life in the Pacific Northwest

Many Native Americans of the Pacific Northwest lived in cedar plank houses. People placed large totem poles in the front of their houses. Totem poles are carved logs that are painted with symbols, called totems.

Food

People used nets made from cedar bark to catch salmon. They caught enough salmon in the spring to last through the winter.

Housing

Most cedar plank houses were built in rows facing the ocean. Each house was home to many families.

Art

Totem poles told stories of important family members or special events. People carved animals, birds, fish, and important places on the poles.

Tribes in the Pacific Northwest did not need to farm because their land was full of natural resources. Cedar trees were one of the most important resources. People used them to make houses, tools, totem poles, and even clothes! Men fished for salmon. It was the most important food.

Practices and Beliefs

People sometimes enjoyed a celebration called a potlatch. They celebrated special occasions with music and dance at a potlatch.

Clothing

During the summer, men wore breechcloths. Women wore skirts and capes made out of woven cedar. They both wore clothes made out of animal skins in the winter. People usually went barefoot, even in the winter!

Reading Skill

Compare and Contrast Compare and contrast the cultures of the tribes of the Pacific Northwest and the Southwest.

1. Circle parts of culture that were the same.

2. Underline the parts that were different.

NGSS Standards SS.2.A.2.2: Compare the cultures of Native American tribes from various geographic regions of the United States.

Lesson 5

? Essential Question How did the natural resources in the Pacific Northwest affect Native Americans?

_____

_____

Go back to *Show As You GO!* on pages 26–27.

networks There's More Online!
● Games ● Assessment

Changing Communities

(t)Digital Vision/Getty Images, (b)John Farmar; Corday Photo Library Ltd./CORBIS

? Essential Question

What changes a community?
What do you think?

_____

_____

_____

_____

Word Hunt

Find and circle these words:

immigrant   settlement

*force

Find two new words.

_____

_____

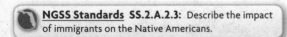 **NGSS Standards SS.2.A.2.3:** Describe the impact of immigrants on the Native Americans.

New Arrivals

At the end of our museum tour, our class met for a discussion. Native Americans were the only people living in America for a long time. Then in 1492, Christopher Columbus arrived in America. **Immigrants** from Europe started coming to America. An immigrant is a person who comes from one country to live in another.

Many immigrants came to build new **settlements** and to find freedom. A settlement is a place that is newly set up as home. The first immigrants to move to America were from Spain.

More and more immigrants kept coming. They started many new settlements. Often the land that they used to create these settlements was home to Native Americans.

At first, Native Americans helped the immigrants. They brought the immigrants food and taught them many things. But as the settlements grew, life changed for the immigrants and Native Americans.

NGSS Standards SS.2.A.2.3: Describe the impact of immigrants on the Native Americans.

Reading Skill

Main Topic and Details Write the main topic and details from the information on pages 54 and 55.

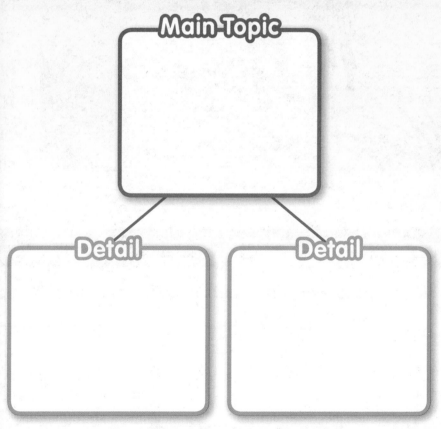

Main Topic

Detail

Detail

Changes for Native Americans

The immigrants learned how to plant their own crops over time. The land they used was often the land that Native Americans used for farming.

As settlements grew, immigrants continued to take more land from Native Americans. Some Native Americans became angry. Soon, fighting started to break out between immigrants and Native Americans. Immigrants continued to **force** many Native Americans from their homes. Some Native American tribes were split apart and forced to move far away.

NGSS Standards SS.2.A.2.3: Describe the impact of immigrants on the Native Americans.

Reading Skill

Sequence **Put the events on pages 56 and 57 in sequence.**

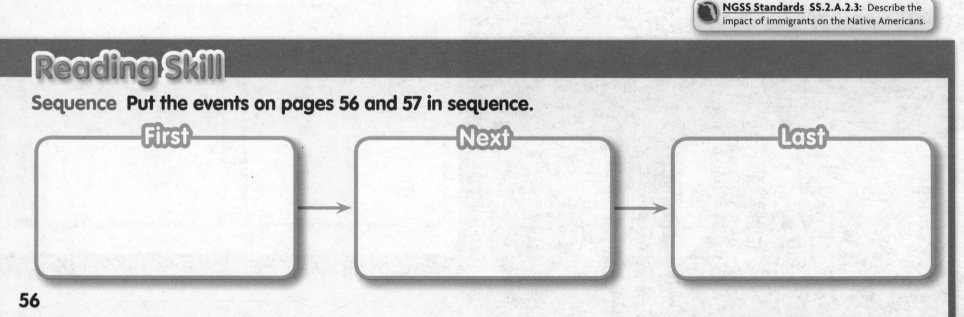

First

Next

Last

Many Native Americans died from diseases brought over by immigrants. Smallpox, measles, and other diseases spread quickly and killed many Native Americans. As more and more immigrants came, life became harder and harder for many Native Americans.

Our class learned so much about Native Americans on our trip to the museum! I am glad I got to share it with you.

NGSS Standards SS.2.A.2.3: Describe the impact of immigrants on the Native Americans.

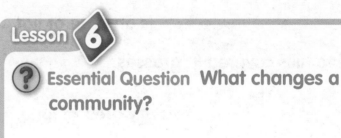

Describe the different ways immigrants had an impact on Native Americans.

_____

_____

_____

_____

_____

Lesson 6

? Essential Question What changes a community?

_____

_____

_____

Go back to *Show As You Go!* on pages 26–27. ◀◀◀

networks **There's More Online!** ● Games ● Assessment

57

UNIT

2 Wrap Up

Who were the first people to live in North America?

To find the answer, fill in the missing word in each sentence. Then write the letters from the circles on the numbered blanks below. Numbers 5 and 13 have been done for you.

> A __r e g i o n__ is an area with
>   9   1
common features that make it different from other areas.

> A __p r a i r i e__ is an area of flat
>   2   4
land or rolling hills covered in grasses.

> A __d e s e r t__ is a dry area of land.
>   6   3

> The beliefs and way of life of a group of people is called __c u l t u r e__.
>   10

> A person who comes from one country to live in another is an __i m m i g r a n t__.
>   11   7

> A place or region that is newly set up as home is called a __s e t t l e m e n t__.
>   8   14

> Plants people grow for food or other uses are __c r o p s__.
>   12   15

__N a t i v e A m e r i c a n s__
 1 2 3 4 5 6 7 8 9 10 11 12 13 14 15

58

Big Idea Project

Make a museum display! Choose one of the Native American regions from the unit. Then make a model showing some examples of daily life in the region. Read the list below to see what you should include in your museum.

My museum display... **Yes it does!**

1. shows three examples of daily life in the region. ○

2. has labels for each example. ○

3. has a label for the region. ○

4. is colorful and detailed. ○

• •

Think About the Big Idea

BIG IDEA 💡 **How does culture influence the way people live?**
Explain in your own words on the lines below.

_____

_____

UNIT 3
A Land of Immigrants

BIG IDEA Change happens over time.

Immigrants from all over the world have been coming to the United States before our country even began. They have shaped the culture of the United States. In this unit, you will learn how these immigrants have changed our country over time.

networks

There's More Online!
- Skill Builders
- Vocabulary Flashcards

Show As You Go!

After you read each lesson in this unit and complete the journal entries, come back to these pages and complete these activities.

Lesson 1

After you read the lesson:

○ Draw a picture of what life was like for you in Colonial America.

Daily life in Colonial America

Lesson 2

After you read the lesson:

- Draw a picture of what you saw as an immigrant arriving at Ellis Island. Be sure to include a caption.

Arrivingat Ellislan

Lesson 3

After you read the lesson:

- Draw a picture of your favorite food that is from a different culture. Be sure to include a caption.

Tokoe   spagetiex   sohex   Toreoke chiken rice

Common Core Standards
R.I.3: Describe the connection between a series of historical events, scientific ideas or concepts, or steps in technical procedures in a text.

Understanding Sequence

Good readers try to understand how ideas are connected in a text. One way authors connect ideas is by sequence. The **sequence** tells the order in which things happen. It tells what happens first, next, and last. Thinking about the order of events will help you understand what you read.

To understand sequence:

1. Look for clue words such as *first, next, later,* and *last*. These words can help show the order of events.

2. Look for dates that tell exactly when things happened.

Paula made a Cuban Sandwich for her friend. First she toasted two slices of bread. Next she spread mustard on one slice of bread and layered it with slices of pork and ham. Then she added melted Swiss cheese and pickles. Last she topped it with a buttered piece of bread and gave it to her friend.

What happened first

What happened next

What happened last

Sergey Kashkin/Getty Images

Try It

You can use the chart below to write events in sequence. Write the events in order from the story on page 62.

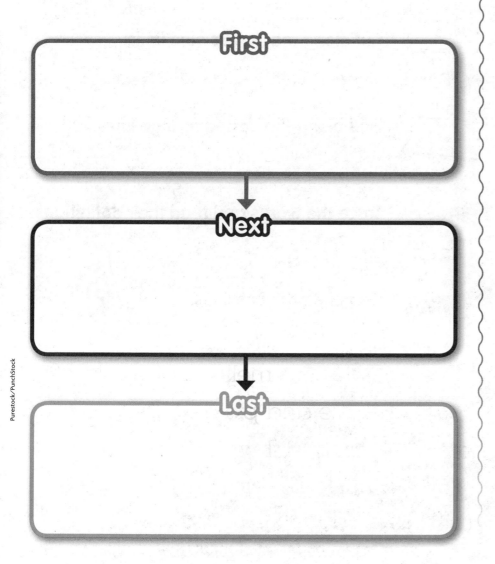

First

Next

Last

Apply It

Now it's your turn to find the sequence! First, read the events of Adam's day below. Then list the events in the proper order.

- Yesterday was Adam's birthday.
- That night Adam blew out candles on his birthday cake.
- During the afternoon Adam had a birthday party at his house.

1. _____

_____

2. _____

_____

3. _____

_____

Purestock/PunchStock

63

Words to Know

Common Core Standards
R.I.4: Determine the meaning of words and phrases in a text relevant to a grade 2 topic or subject area.

The list below shows some important words you will learn in this unit. Their definitions can be found on the next page. Read the words.

colony p. 68

colonist p. 69

Statue of Liberty p. 76

Ellis Island p. 77

contribution p. 81

custom p. 81

FOLDABLES®

The Foldable on the next page will help you learn these important words. Follow the steps below to make your Foldable.

Step 1 Cut along the dotted blue lines.

Step 2 Fold along the dotted orange lines.

Step 3 Trace the words and read their definitions.

Step 4  Complete the activities.

(l)Lee Nelson, (r)Library of Congress, Prints and Photographs Division [LC-USZ62-37784]

Long ago, America was ruled by a country called England. America was a _____ of England.

Write key words from the definition to help you remember the meaning of the word colonist.

_____

_____

Is Ellis Island a person, place, or thing?

_____

A **colony** is a place that is ruled by another country.

A **colonist** is a person who travels to a new land in order to settle it.

Ellis Island was an important immigration center in the United States.

The **Statue of Liberty** is a statue of a woman holding a torch.

A **contribution** is the act of giving or doing something.

A **custom** is a special way of doing something that is shared by many people.

Draw a picture of the Statue of Liberty.

What contribution can you make to keep your classroom clean?

_____

_____

What is a custom you share with your family?

_____

_____

Statue of
Liberty

Fold Here

contribution

custom

Fold Here

colony

colonist

Ellis Island

Primary Sources

NGSS Standards
SS.2.A.1.1: Examine primary and secondary sources.

Photographs are one type of primary source. A photograph is a picture that is taken with a camera. People have been using cameras and taking pictures for many years. Photographs from long ago can show us what life was like way back then. We can learn about how people lived and the places they went long ago.

This is a photograph of immigrants arriving at Ellis Island in 1904.

 Document-Based Questions

1. **What do you see going on in this photograph?**

_____

_____

2. **How can you tell this photograph is from long ago?**

_____

networks
There's More Online!
● Skill Builders
● Resource Library

1 Colonial America

? Essential Question

How do communities change over time?

What do you think?

_____

_____

_____

Word Hunt

Find and (circle) these words:

colony   *ruled

colonist

Find 2 more new words:

_____

_____

NGSS Standards SS.2.A.2.4: Explore ways the daily life of people living in Colonial America changed over time.

The First Colonists

It was Presentation Day in Mrs. Jones's class. Sophia was the first to present. She told the class about the first immigrants who came to America long ago.

"Over time many immigrants moved to America from Europe," Sophia said. She told the class that many of the first immigrants came from England. They settled all along the eastern coast of America. As the settlements grew, they became known as colonies. Sophia explained that a **colony** is a place that is ruled by another country. The colonies in America were **ruled** by England. The rules colonists in America had to follow were made by England.

Sophia explained to the class that the immigrants who settled in America were known as **colonists**. A colonist is a person who travels to a new land to settle it. The first groups of colonists faced many problems. They were not familiar with the new land. Some colonists had a hard time growing food in their new land. Sometimes their food supplies ran out during the winter. It was a hard life for the first colonists.

Why was life hard for the colonists at first?

_____

_____

_____

_____

_____

NGSS Standards **SS.2.A.2.4:** Explore ways the daily life of people living in Colonial America changed over time.

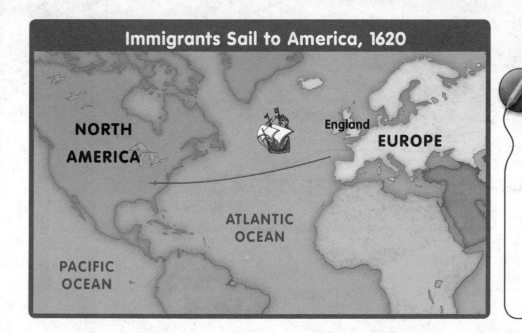

Immigrants Sail to America, 1620

NORTH AMERICA

England

EUROPE

ATLANTIC OCEAN

PACIFIC OCEAN

Map and Globe Skills

1. In what direction did the immigrants coming from Europe sail?

_____

2. Near what ocean did the immigrants settle?

_____

69

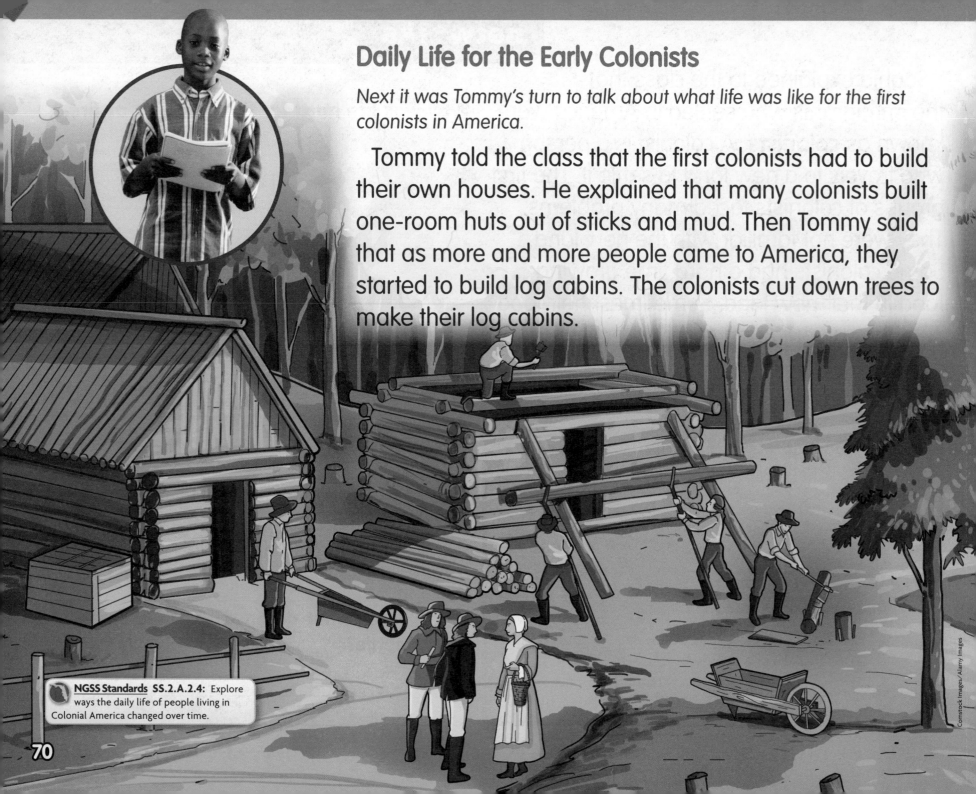

Daily Life for the Early Colonists

Next it was Tommy's turn to talk about what life was like for the first colonists in America.

Tommy told the class that the first colonists had to build their own houses. He explained that many colonists built one-room huts out of sticks and mud. Then Tommy said that as more and more people came to America, they started to build log cabins. The colonists cut down trees to make their log cabins.

NGSS Standards SS.2.A.2.4: Explore ways the daily life of people living in Colonial America changed over time.

Comstock Images/Alamy Images

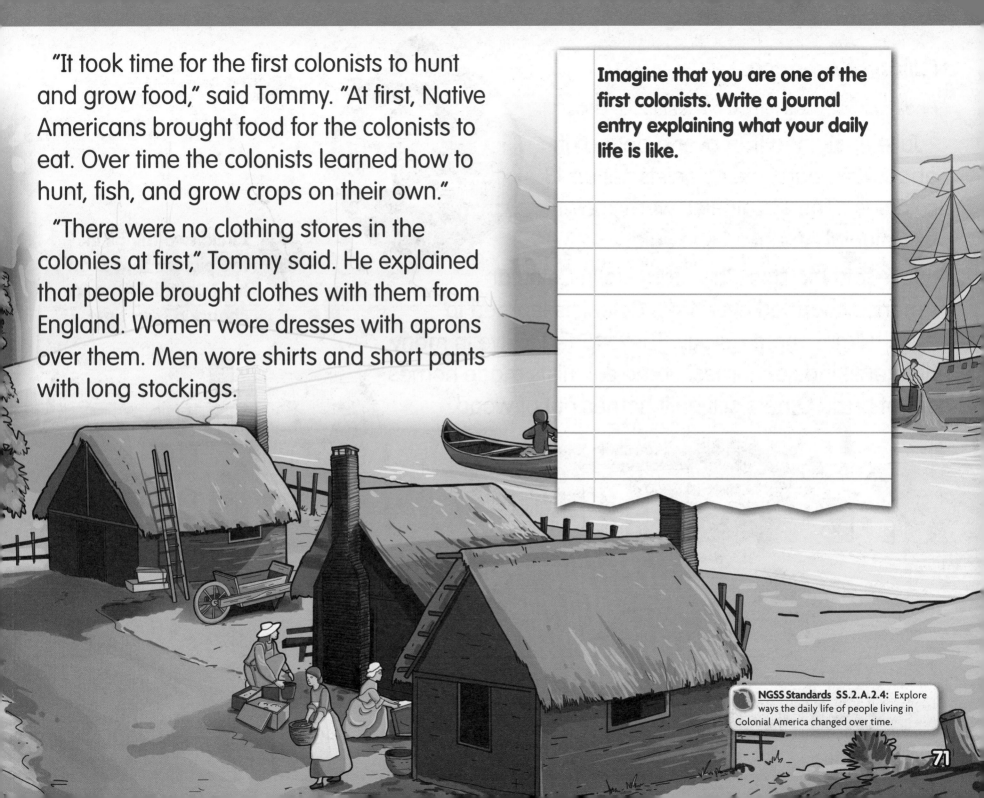

"It took time for the first colonists to hunt and grow food," said Tommy. "At first, Native Americans brought food for the colonists to eat. Over time the colonists learned how to hunt, fish, and grow crops on their own."

"There were no clothing stores in the colonies at first," Tommy said. He explained that people brought clothes with them from England. Women wore dresses with aprons over them. Men wore shirts and short pants with long stockings.

Imagine that you are one of the first colonists. Write a journal entry explaining what your daily life is like.

NGSS Standards SS.2.A.2.4: Explore ways the daily life of people living in Colonial America changed over time.

71

Colonial America

Finally it was Julie's turn to present to the class.

Julie explained that over a period of about 100 years, the colonists set up 13 colonies. "The 13 colonies were known as Colonial America," she said.

Julie told the class that daily life in Colonial America changed over time. Colonists learned to build homes more quickly. They started to live in many different kinds of homes. Some colonists made homes out of brick. Others still built homes out of wood.

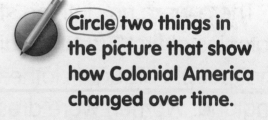

NGSS Standards SS.2.A.2.4: Explore ways the daily life of people living in Colonial America changed over time. **SS.2.A.3.1:** Identify terms and designations of time sequence.

Circle two things in the picture that show how Colonial America changed over time.

Ryan McVay/Getty Images

72

Julie explained that many colonists started to grow vegetables in gardens or on farms near their houses. Many people had dairy barns and chicken coops close to their homes. Some women started to wear fancy dresses. Men started to wear shoes with buckles.

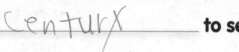

Time Sequence		
12 months	=	1 year
10 years	=	1 decade
100 years	=	1 century

Look at the chart above. It took the colonists one

_____Century_____ **to set up the 13 colonies.**

NGSS Standards SS.2.A.2.4: Explore ways the daily life of people living in Colonial America changed over time. **SS.2.A.3.1:** Identify terms and designations of time sequence.

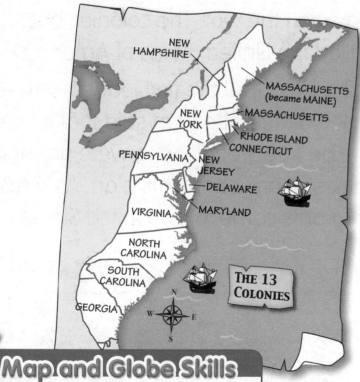

NEW HAMPSHIRE

MASSACHUSETTS (became MAINE)

NEW YORK

MASSACHUSETTS

RHODE ISLAND
CONNECTICUT

PENNSYLVANIA

NEW JERSEY

DELAWARE

VIRGINIA

MARYLAND

NORTH CAROLINA

SOUTH CAROLINA

THE 13 COLONIES

GEORGIA

N W E S

Map and Globe Skills

Color the colony that is directly north of Georgia.

Lesson 1

? **Essential Question How do communities change over time?**

_____

_____

_____

Go back to *Show As You Go!* **on pages 60–61.**

netw⊙rks **There's More Online!**
● Games ● Assessment

Coming to America

? **Essential Question**

Why do people move?
What do you think?

_____

_____

_____

_____

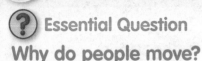

Word Hunt

Find and circle these words:

*escape   Ellis Island

Statue of Liberty

Find 2 more new words:

_____

_____

NGSS Standards SS.2.A.2.5: Identify reasons
people came to the United States throughout history.

The United States of America

immigration

The next week, it was Presentation Day for more students. Anthony was the first to present.

"In 1775, the colonists went to war with England to fight for their freedom," said Anthony. He explained that the colonists won the war. The colonies became a new country called the United States of America.

Anthony told the class that the first leaders wrote a plan for the United States. The plan said that all people have the right to be free. People who were unhappy in their own countries heard about this plan. As a result, millions of immigrants came to the United States.

"There were many reasons immigrants came to the United States," said Anthony. In the United States, they would have the freedom to choose their own way of life. For example, they would have the freedom to choose their own religion. They would also be able to buy their own land.

Anthony explained that other immigrants came to **escape** war. For them, the United States was a place of safety. Some immigrants came to find jobs. Others came to escape hunger in their home countries. Their hopes of a better life gave them courage to make the journey across the ocean.

Immigrants arrive in the United States.

Underline the reasons immigrants came to America.

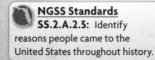
NGSS Standards
SS.2.A.2.5: Identify reasons people came to the United States throughout history.

Reading Skill

Determine the Meaning of Unknown Words
Sometimes, you may not understand the meaning of a word. When this happens, read the story again and look for clues.
What does this word mean?

escape: _____

_____

75

Arriving in the United States

Next it was Lena's turn to present her report.

Lena said that between the years 1892 and 1954, millions of immigrants came to the United States. Many came in ships through New York Harbor. As the immigrants entered the harbor, they could see the **Statue of Liberty**.

"The Statue of Liberty is a large statue that was a gift from France. It is located on Liberty Island in New York Harbor," said Lena. "The Statue of Liberty stands for the freedoms we have in the United States."

NGSS Standards
SS.2.A.2.6: Discuss the importance of Ellis Island and the Statue of Liberty to immigration from 1892–1954.

Statue of Liberty

Ellis Island

New York

"The first place many immigrants went before they began their lives in America was **Ellis Island**," said Lena. "Ellis Island was an important immigration center in New York Harbor. The center was opened on January 1, 1892, so that immigration officials could find out how many people were arriving in America."

The Statue of Liberty was shipped from France in pieces and put together in the United States. It took over four months to finish!

Imagine you are an immigrant arriving in New York Harbor. Write a journal entry telling what you see and feel. Explain why the Statue of Liberty is important to you.

I would be happy and sad. I would be happy for what it stans for. I would be sad beacus I would miss my houes.

NGSS Standards SS.2.A.2.6: Discuss the importance of Ellis Island and the Statue of Liberty to immigration from 1892–1954.

NGSS Standards
SS.2.A.2.6: Discuss the importance of Ellis Island and the Statue of Liberty to immigration from 1892–1954.

The Ellis Island Experience

Next it was Ethan's turn to present about Ellis Island.

Ethan told the class that on Ellis Island, immigrants had to go through many steps before they could enter the United States. First, they were given an exam by doctors. The doctors had to make sure immigrants were not sick. People who were sick had to stay at Ellis Island to be treated.

"Next, the immigrants were asked a list of questions like: What is your name? What country are you from? If the immigrants passed the health exam and answered the questions, they were given entry cards," said Ethan. "Finally, most were able to enter the United States."

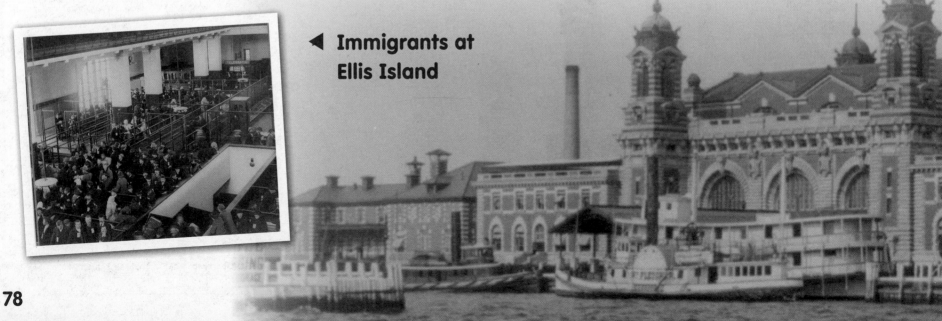

◄ **Immigrants at Ellis Island**

Ethan explained that from 1892 to 1954, millions of immigrants passed through Ellis Island. Eventually the United States began to limit the number of immigrants that could come into the country. As a result, Ellis Island was no longer as busy as it had been. In 1954 it was closed. Today it is a museum that reminds people of the immigrant experience in the United States.

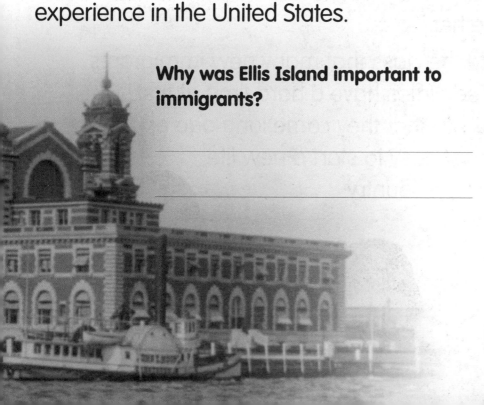

Why was Ellis Island important to immigrants?

_____

_____

Understand Sequence **Place an immigrant's experience at Ellis Island in sequence. Number the boxes below in the correct order.**

exam by a doctor	asked questions	received entry card	arrived at Ellis Island
2	3	4	1

NGSS Standards SS.2.A.2.6: Discuss the importance of Ellis Island and the Statue of Liberty to immigration from 1892–1954.

Lesson 2

? Essential Question Why do people move?

_____

_____

_____

Go back to *Show As You Go!* on pages 60–61. ⟪

netw⬤rks connected.mcgraw-hill.com
⬤ Games ⬤ Assessment

Sharing Culture

(t)Thomas Northcut/Photodisc/Getty Images. (b)Kevin Dodge/CORBIS. (inset)Hill Street Studios/Blend Images/Getty Images

? **Essential Question**

How does culture shape a community?

What do you think?

_____

_____

_____

Word Hunt

Find and (circle) these words:

*blend   contribution

custom

Find 2 more new words:

_____

_____

NGSS Standards **SS.2.A.2.7:** Discuss why immigration continues today. **SS.2.A.2.8:** Explain the cultural influences and contributions of immigrants today.

Immigration Today

"This is the final week of presentations!" said Mrs. Jones. It was Paula's turn to present.

"Many immigrants still move to the United States every year," said Paula. "Today, immigrants come to the United States from all over the world." Paula explained that all immigrants have shaped the United States as a place where many cultures **blend** together.

Paula told the class that many new immigrants to the United States have a hard time at first. This is true whether they came long ago or today. It is not easy to start a new life in a brand new country.

"No matter where immigrants come from, most move to the United States in search of a better life," said Paula. "Many still come to find jobs. Others still come to escape war and hunger in their home countries. Religious freedom also continues to be a reason why immigrants come to the United States today."

Paula told the class that immigrants have made many **contributions** to our country. A contribution is the act of giving or doing something. Over time, the beliefs and **customs** of different immigrant groups have added to the culture in the United States. A custom is a special way of doing something that is shared by many people. For instance, many families celebrate birthdays with cake.

1. Circle the reasons why immigration continues today.

2. What is a custom that you share with your family?

_____

A birthday custom

NGSS Standards **SS.2.A.2.7:** Discuss why immigration continues today. **SS.2.A.2.8:** Explain the cultural influences and contributions of immigrants today.

Purestock/PunchStock

Learning New Customs

Paula continued with her presentation. She had researched how other cultures have added to the culture of the United States.

Paula took pictures of things she saw in her neighborhood. She made a poster to show how other cultures have influenced things like food, music, clothing, art, language, and celebrations.

This picture shows an Italian restaurant in our neighborhood. Long ago, Americans did not eat spaghetti. Immigrants from Italy made it popular in our country. Today Americans enjoy making spaghetti at home and eating it in restaurants.

(l)Ryan Pierse/Stone/Getty Images, (r)Michael Lamotte/Cole Group/Getty Images

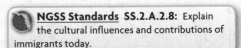

NGSS Standards SS.2.A.2.8: Explain the cultural influences and contributions of immigrants today.

Think about other foods, music, and clothing from different cultures. Describe one of them in a journal entry.

My family and I took a walk in our neighborhood, and we noticed a group of people playing jazz music. Africans who came to the United States brought songs and rhythms with them. Musicians in the United States changed the music and turned it into jazz. Jazz, blues, and hip hop are just some of the kinds of music we listen to today that grew out of African music.

Mrs. Ross, our librarian, was wearing a shirt made out of silk. Silk cloth was invented in China. Many Chinese immigrants brought silk with them when they came to the United States. Silk is very soft and is used today to make clothing.

83

My family and I went to a Caribbean carnival downtown. It was so colorful! People were dressed in costumes and dancing. Long ago, people in the Caribbean Islands danced through their villages in costumes. Today people enjoy practicing this tradition at carnivals around the world.

I went to the Miami Art Museum with my family. I noticed some paintings that were made by an African American artist named Jacob Lawrence. He was inspired by African art, which typically uses flat shapes and bright colors. He borrowed these ideas and made them a part of his work.

Write down something that you learned from Paula's presentation.

_____

_____

_____

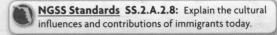

NGSS Standards **SS.2.A.2.8:** Explain the cultural influences and contributions of immigrants today.

When I was walking home from school last week someone asked if I had seen their missing Chihuahua. I had never heard of a Chihuahua. The person said a Chihuahua is a kind of dog. The name comes from a state in Mexico. This is an example of a Mexican word that we use in our language today.

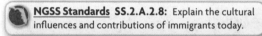

NGSS Standards SS.2.A.2.8: Explain the cultural influences and contributions of immigrants today.

"Some customs are brought to the United States by immigrants. Other customs are created right here," said Paula. "Together these customs from near and far mix and make one big culture that we all share. In fact, the United States has one of the most diverse cultures on Earth!"

The class clapped for Paula at the end of her presentation. Mrs. Jones told everyone that they had done a wonderful job teaching each other.

Dex Image/Getty Images

Lesson 3

? Essential Question How does culture shape a community?

_____

_____

_____

Go back to *Show As You Go!* on pages 60–61.

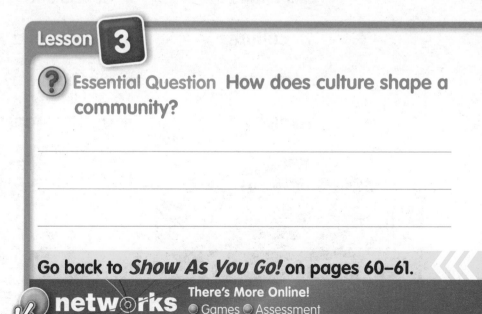

networks There's More Online!
● Games ● Assessment

Match each word with its definition.

custom   ● a person who travels to a new land to settle it

colony   ● a person who comes from another country to live in another

Statue of Liberty   ● a place that is ruled by another country

colonist   ● the act of giving or doing something

Ellis Island   ● beliefs and way of life of a group of people

culture   ● a statue of a woman holding a torch

contribution   ● a special way of doing something that is shared by people

immigrant   ● an important immigration center in the United States

Big Idea Project

Think about your culture. Make a poster that shows some of the things that make up your culture. Read the list below to see what you should include on your poster. As you work, check off each task as you complete it.

My poster...	Yes it does!
1. shows food and clothing	○
2. shows music and art	○
3. shows a celebration	○
4. is colorful and detailed	○

Think About the Big Idea

BIG IDEA 💡 How does change happen over time?
Explain the answer in your own words on the lines below.

_____

_____

4 Citizens and Government

People's actions can help or hurt others. Think about a time when your actions affected another person. In this unit, you will learn about being a responsible citizen who helps others and follows rules. You will also learn how rules and laws keep people safe and help us to get along.

connected.mcgraw-hill.com
● Skill Builders
● Vocabulary Flashcards

Show As You Go!

After you read each lesson in this unit, complete the activities to practice what you are learning!

Lesson 1

After you read the lesson:

○ How do people become citizens of the United States?

Becoming a Citizen

People who are born in the United States are American citizens, an

Lesson 2

After you read the lesson:

○ What are some rights and responsibilities of United States citizens?

Rights and Responsibilities

right to vote
freedom of speech
freedom of religion.

(corkboard)The McGraw-Hill Companies

Lesson 3

After you read the lesson:

○ Tell about the contributions of a special American.

Contributions of a Special American

Mary McLeod Bethune, she helped African girls go to school and get edu

Lesson 4

After you read the lesson:

○ Why do people form governments?

○ What could happen if we did not have rules?

People form governments to

If we didn't have rules, people could

Lesson 5

After you read the lesson:

 Draw or glue a picture of a symbol of the United States. Label it.

An American Symbol

Reading Skill

Common Core Standards
RI.6: Identify what the author wants to answer, explain, or describe in the text.
RI.8: Describe how reasons support specific points the author makes in a text.

Author's Purpose

An author is a person who writes stories and other texts. Authors have a purpose for writing. The purpose may be to answer, explain, or describe something.

When you read, it is important to think about the author's purpose and the reasons that support it. This will help you focus on what you should understand about the text.

 Learn It

To find the author's purpose and reasons to support it:

1. **Read the text.**
2. **Decide what the author wants to describe, explain, or answer.**
3. **Read the text again. Look for reasons that support the author's purpose.**

My name is Carlos. I am moving to America. My parents chose to move for better jobs. We will be able to buy a house. My parents hope to make a better life for our family in America.

> **This sentence tells what the author wants to explain.**

> **These sentences are the reasons Carlos is moving to America.**

Bruce Laurance/Blend Images/Getty Images

List the author's purpose and reasons from the text on page 90 in the chart below.

Author's Purpose

```
┌─────────────────────┐
│                     │
│                     │
│                     │
└─────────────────────┘
```

Reason

```
┌──────────────┐        ┌──────────────┐
│              │        │              │
│              │        │              │
└──────────────┘        └──────────────┘
```

Reason

```
┌──────────────┐
│              │
│              │
└──────────────┘
```

John Wang/Getty Images

- **Read the letter below. Who is the author of the letter?**

  _____

- **Circle what the author wants to describe.**

- **Underline the reasons that support what the author wants to describe.**

Dear Manuel,

I saw the Statue of Liberty today! It is in New York City. The statue is 305 feet tall. Did you know the Statue of Liberty welcomes people to America?

Your friend,
Carlos

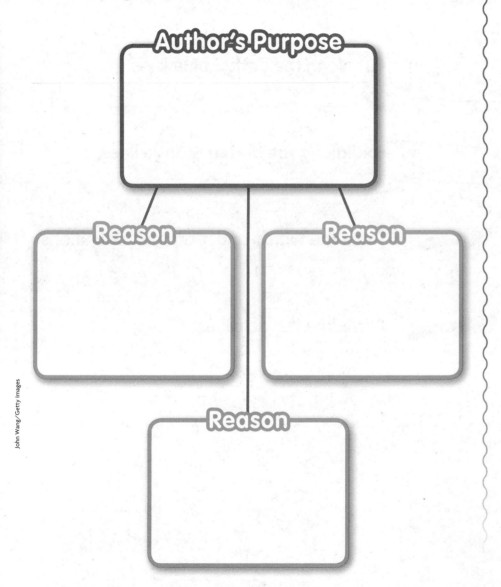

Words to Know

The list below shows some important words you will learn in this unit. Their definitions can be found on the next page. Read the words.

citizen p. 96

rights p. 100

volunteer p. 104

recycle p. 105

government p. 114

Constitution p. 116

FOLDABLES®

The Foldable on the next page will help you learn these important words. Follow the steps below to make your Foldable.

Step 1 Cut along the dotted blue lines.

Step 2 Fold along the dotted orange lines.

Step 3 Trace the words and read their definitions.

Step 4 Complete the activities.

(l)Comstock, (r)Photodisc/Getty Images

Finish the sentence.
I am a citizen of

_____.

Circle a right or freedom you have.

- I can take things that do not belong to me.

- I can go to school.

Write the name of a person who is a volunteer at your school.

_____

A **citizen** is a person who belongs to a country.

Rights are freedoms people have.

A **volunteer** is a person who works for free to help others.

To **recycle** means to reuse something.

A **government** is all of the people who run a community, state, or country.

The **Constitution** is a plan for our government.

What kinds of things can be recycled?

_____

Cross out the word that does not belong with government.

mayor   governor

President   baker

The Constitution has important laws. What is a law that you follow?

_____

_____

93

recycle | government | Constitution

Fold Here

citizen | rights | volunteer

Fold Here

Primary Sources

NGSS Standards
SS.2.A.1.1: Examine primary and secondary sources.

Documents are a type of primary source. A document is a paper that gives information. The document pictured here is the Constitution of the United States.

Audio and video recordings are also sources of information. They have sound and moving pictures. The video recording pictured here is a secondary source. A secondary source is something that is made or written after an event happens. This video recording is about the Constitution.

 Document-Based Questions

1. **How can you tell the first three words of the Constitution are important?**

_____

2. **Why do you think this video recording about the Constitution was made?**

_____

networks
There's More Online!
● Skill Builders
● Resource Library

95

United States Citizens

? Essential Question

What does it mean to belong to a country?

What do you think?

_____

_____

_____

Word Hunt

Find and circle these words:

citizen   naturalization

*introduce

Find 2 more new words:

_____

_____

NGSS Standards SS.2.C.2.1: Identify what it means to be a United States citizen either by birth or by naturalization.

Becoming a Citizen

It was Carlos's first day in his new school. His teacher, Mrs. Miller, **introduced** him to the class. She told the students that Carlos and his parents had just become **citizens** of the United States. A citizen is a person who belongs to a country.

Mrs. Miller explained to the class how people become citizens.

★ People who are born in the United States are American citizens.

★ People also become citizens through **naturalization**. Naturalization is when a person becomes a citizen of another country.

Bruce Laurance/Blend Images/Getty Images

"Many of the students in our class were born in the United States," said Mrs. Miller. "Some students, like Carlos, were born in another country." Mrs. Miller asked the students to introduce themselves to Carlos and tell him where they were born.

Introduce yourself to Carlos!

My name is _Madiosn_

I was born in _____

Draw or glue a picture of yourself here.

Jose Luis Pelaez/Getty Images

Draw boxes around the two ways people become citizens.

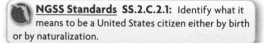
NGSS Standards SS.2.C.2.1: Identify what it means to be a United States citizen either by birth or by naturalization.

97

The next day, Carlos brought his scrapbook to school. He wanted to show the class how he had become a citizen.

How I Became a United States Citizen by Carlos

Tijuana
Ciudad Juárez
Monterrey
Gulf of California
Gulf of Mexico
PACIFIC OCEAN
MEXICO
Guadalajara
Mexico City

N
W E
S
0   250   500 miles
0   250   500 kilometers

I was born in Mexico.

Pensacola
Tallahassee
Jacksonville
ATLANTIC OCEAN
N
W E
S
Gulf of Mexico
Orlando
FLORIDA
Tampa
Miami
Florida Keys

0   100   200 miles
0   100   200 kilometers

We moved to Florida. My parents chose to become United States citizens.

NGSS Standards SS.2.C.2.1: Identify what it means to be a United States citizen either by birth or by naturalization.

98

My parents became citizens through naturalization.

- First, they signed papers saying they wanted to be citizens of the United States.

- Next, they took classes in English, American history, and citizenship.

- Then, they took a test to show what they learned.

- Last, my parents went to a special ceremony and pledged to be loyal citizens.

NGSS Standards SS.2.C.2.1: Identify what it means to be a United States citizen either by birth or by naturalization.

DID YOU KNOW?
Children do not need to go through the steps of naturalization. When their parents become citizens, they do too!

Draw a picture of Carlos with the American flag.

Comstock

Lesson **1**

? Essential Question What does it mean to belong to a country?

You could be freer

Go back to *Show As You Go!* on page 88–89.

? Essential Question

What does it mean to be a citizen?
What do you think?

_____

_____

_____

_____

_____

_____

Word Hunt

Find and (circle) these words:

rights   responsible

*positive   volunteer

recycle

NGSS Standards SS.2.C.2.3: Explain why United States citizens have guaranteed rights and identify rights.

Guaranteed Rights

Later that day, Mrs. Miller taught the students about the guaranteed **rights**, or freedoms, of United States citizens. Guaranteed means that no one can take these rights away. Read on to learn about some of these rights.

United States citizens have the right to vote.

Bob Daemmrich/PhotoEdit

The right to vote means citizens can choose their leaders.

United States citizens have the freedom of speech.

United States citizens also have the freedom of religion.

The freedom of speech means that citizens are free to say what they think.

The freedom of religion means that citizens are free to worship as they choose.

Mrs. Miller explained to the students that these guaranteed rights are very important to Americans. Many people come to America because of these freedoms.

THINK · PAIR · SHARE
Why are guaranteed rights important to Americans?

(Circle) three guaranteed rights of United States citizens.

NGSS Standards **SS.2.C.2.3:** Explain why United States citizens have guaranteed rights and identify rights.

Responsible Citizenship

"I want to be the best citizen I can be!" said Carlos. "We do too!" exclaimed Carlos's classmates. Mrs. Miller told the class that it is important for citizens to be **responsible**. Responsible means able to choose between right and wrong. The students talked about how they planned to be responsible citizens.

Circle the words that describe how responsible citizens act.

I will show *respect* towards people and their property by using kind words and actions. I will also help people at school and in my neighborhood.

Susan Hestir/Gibbs Magnet School of International Studies and Foreign Languages

NGSS Standards
SS.2.C.2.2: Define and apply the characteristics of responsible citizenship.

I will be *self-reliant.* That means that I will be responsible for getting my work done at school. At home, I will do my homework and chores without being asked.

I will be a responsible citizen by *participating*, or taking part, in "Community Clean Up Day." It is *patriotic* to help in your community. Patriotic means showing respect and love for your country.

I will be a responsible citizen by being *honest*. I will be truthful and fair.

How will you be a responsible citizen? Write your plan on the lines below.

_____

_____

_____

_____

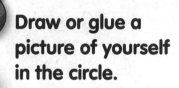

Draw or glue a picture of yourself in the circle.

(l)Sarah Nasim/Brier Creek Elementary School, (r)Susan Hestir/Gibbs Magnet School of International Studies and Foreign Languages

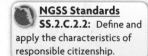

NGSS Standards
SS.2.C.2.2: Define and apply the characteristics of responsible citizenship.

Taking Action

"Responsible citizens also make contributions to make our country a better place to live," said Mrs. Miller. A contribution is something a person does to help others. One way citizens can make a **positive** contribution is by being a **volunteer**. A volunteer is a person who works for free to help others. How are the volunteers in these pictures helping others?

 NGSS Standards SS.2.C.2.4: Identify ways citizens can make a positive contribution in their community.

 Write a caption for each picture.

Plant a tree

Tutoring

Picking up Trash

"I know another way we can help our community!" said Lin. "We can **recycle**!" To recycle means to reuse something. Glass, plastic, and newspapers can be recycled and made into something else. Recycling helps protect our environment.

What is another way to make a positive contribution to your community?

_____

_____

NGSS Standards SS.2.C.2.4: Identify ways citizens can make a positive contribution in their community.

Ariel Skelley/Blend Images/Getty Images

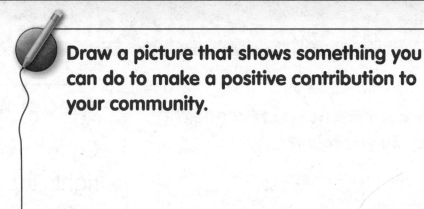

Draw a picture that shows something you can do to make a positive contribution to your community.

Lesson 2

Essential Question What does it mean to be a citizen?

_____

_____

_____

Go back to *Show As You Go!* on pages 88–89. ⫸

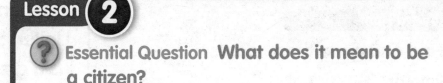

netw⬤rks

There's More Online!
⬤ Games ⬤ Assessment

Citizens Create Change

? Essential Question

How can citizens create change?

What do you think?

_____

_____

_____

_____

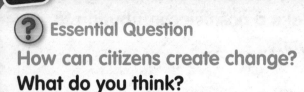

Word Hunt

Find and (circle) these words:

veteran   *equal

Find 2 more new words.

_____

_____

NGSS Standards SS.2.C.2.3: Explain why United States citizens have guaranteed rights and identify rights.
SS.2.C.2.5: Evaluate the contributions of various African Americans, Hispanics, Native Americans, veterans, and women.

Special Americans

Carlos wondered why United States citizens have rights that people in some other countries do not have. Carlos's classmates told him about the contributions of special people who worked hard for the rights of United States citizens.

Lily taught Carlos about George Washington.

"George Washington led America in the war for independence. He became the first President of the United States. George Washington is remembered as a great leader and an important **veteran**. A veteran is a person who has been in the military."

Why were George Washington's contributions important?

He helped America become a free country.

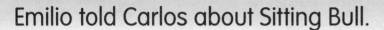
Emilio told Carlos about Sitting Bull.

"Sitting Bull was a Lakota Native American chief. He lived at a time when many Native Americans were forced away from their land to make room for the immigrants. Sitting Bull knew this was not fair. He fought to keep Native Americans from losing their land. Sitting Bull was a brave leader. "

Why were Sitting Bull's contributions important?

He fought to keep Native Americans from losing their land.

NGSS Standards SS.2.A.1.1: Examine primary and secondary sources.
SS.2.C.2.3: Explain why United States citizens have guaranteed rights and identify rights. **SS.2.C.2.5:** Evaluate the contributions of various African Americans, Hispanics, Native Americans, veterans, and women.

DID YOU KNOW?
A quarter is a primary source. Quarters have a picture of George Washington on them.

Reading Skill

Author's Purpose When you read, it is a good idea to think about what the author wants to answer, explain, or describe.

What is the purpose of the paragraph on this page?

If tells you to stand up to uters and Jest because thay

Natalie talked about Susan B. Anthony.

"Years ago women in our country did not have **equal** rights. They were not allowed to vote. Susan B. Anthony knew this was not fair. She talked to lawmakers. She led marches and gave speeches. Susan worked hard for a new law that allowed women to vote."

NGSS Standards SS.2.C.2.3: Explain why United States citizens have guaranteed rights and identify rights. SS.2.C.2.5: Evaluate the contributions of various African Americans, Hispanics, Native Americans, veterans, and women.

Why were Susan B. Anthony's contributions important?

She Worked hard to get a law passed so that womem could vote.

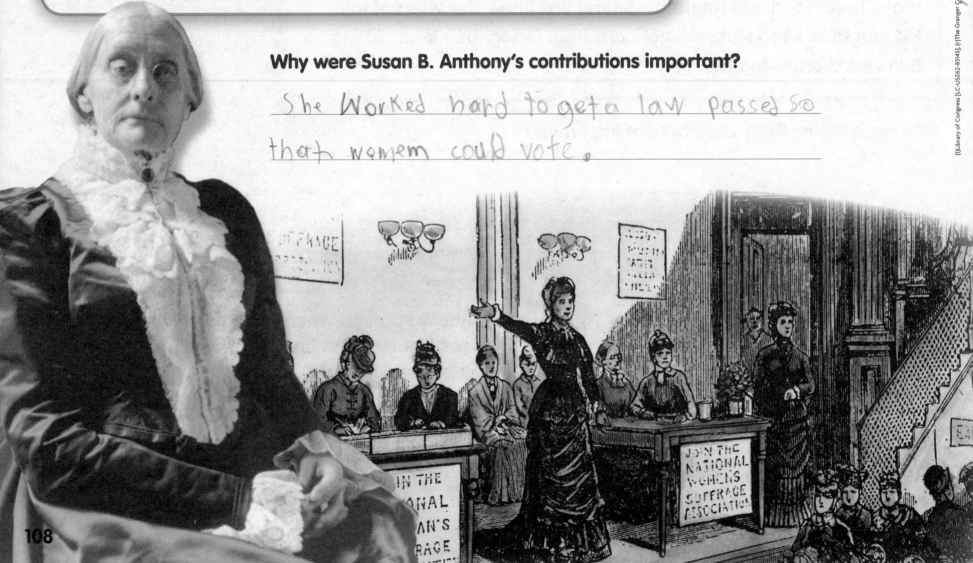

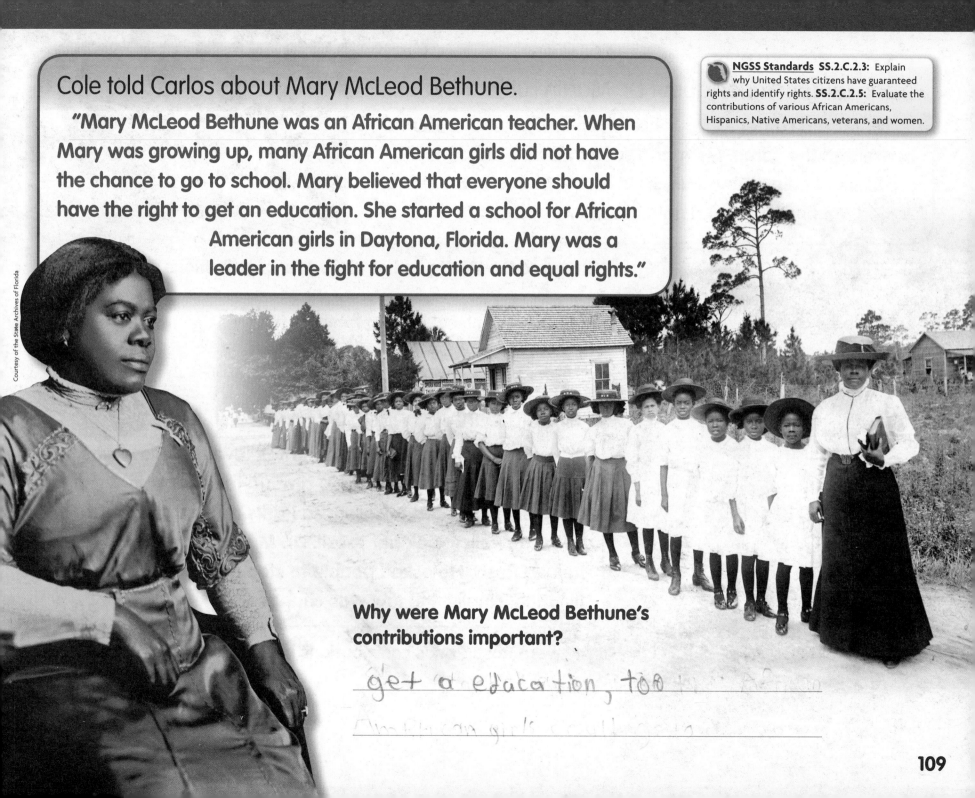

Cole told Carlos about Mary McLeod Bethune.

"Mary McLeod Bethune was an African American teacher. When Mary was growing up, many African American girls did not have the chance to go to school. Mary believed that everyone should have the right to get an education. She started a school for African American girls in Daytona, Florida. Mary was a leader in the fight for education and equal rights."

NGSS Standards SS.2.C.2.3: Explain why United States citizens have guaranteed rights and identify rights. SS.2.C.2.5: Evaluate the contributions of various African Americans, Hispanics, Native Americans, veterans, and women.

Courtesy of the State Archives of Florida

Why were Mary McLeod Bethune's contributions important?

get a education, too

American girls

109

Sean taught Carlos about Dr. Martin Luther King, Jr.

"Dr. Martin Luther King, Jr., believed that everyone should be treated the same. He made speeches and led peaceful marches to help change unfair laws. Dr. Martin Luther King, Jr., led the fight for equal rights for all Americans."

NGSS Standards **SS.2.C.2.3:** Explain why United States citizens have guaranteed rights and identify rights. **SS.2.C.2.5:** Evaluate the contributions of various African Americans, Hispanics, Native Americans, veterans, and women.

Why were Dr. Martin Luther King, Jr.'s, contributions important?

He thought everyone sould be theated equally.

Lin told Carlos about Rosa Parks.

"Years ago, many states had unfair laws. One law was that African Americans had to give up their seats to white people on crowded buses. Rosa Parks refused to give up her seat. Police took her to jail. Dr. Martin Luther King, Jr., helped Rosa. He asked people to stop riding buses. People listened. Finally, the law was changed."

Bettmann/CORBIS

Why were Rosa Park's contributions important?

She help get rid of unfair laws.

Ben taught Carlos about César Chávez.

"César Chávez was a famous Hispanic leader. He worked to make life better for farm workers. Laws said that farm workers did not have to be treated the same as other workers. They had to work long hours and were paid very little money. César Chávez gave speeches and led marches to change these laws. His actions helped farm workers to have more rights."

Why were César Chávez's contributions important?

He help farms to get equal rights.

NGSS Standards SS.2.A.1.2: Utilize the media center, technology, or other informational sources to locate information that provides answers to questions about a historical topic.

Media Center

Use the Internet and other sources to find out:

1. **What is the name of the speech Dr. Martin Luther King, Jr., made on August 28, 1963?**

_____

2. **When did Susan B. Anthony and other women in the United States get the right to vote?**

_____

Lesson 3

? **Essential Question** How can citizens create change?

They can give speeches, call or write to lawmakers.

Go back to *Show As You Go!* on pages 88–89.

networks There's More Online!
● Games ● Assessment

Rules and Laws

? Essential Question

How do people get along?

What do you think?

_____

_____

_____

_____

_____

Find and circle these words:

government   Constitution

*structure   *function

We Need Rules

The next day the students explained their classroom rules to Carlos. The students talked about what would happen if they did not follow each rule.

The students agreed that rules are important. Rules at home and at school keep people safe. Rules also help people to be good citizens. Without rules, things would be out of control and people could get hurt.

1. What is a rule that you have in your home or classroom?

_____

_____

2. Why is the rule important?

_____

_____

Digital Vision/Getty Images

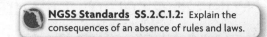

THINK · PAIR · SHARE

The students made a chart to show their classroom rules. Look at the chart below. Write what you think would happen if students did not follow each rule.

NGSS Standards SS.2.C.1.2: Explain the consequences of an absence of rules and laws.

Our Classroom Rules		
Classroom Rule	**Reason we have this rule:**	**What would happen if students did not follow this rule?**
1. Raise your hand and wait to be called on before speaking out.	This rule helps everyone get a chance to speak in class.	
2. Keep hands, feet, and objects to yourself.	This rule helps keep students safe.	
3. Walk in the classroom and school building. Do not run!	This rule helps keep students, teachers, and visitors safe.	

Our Government

NGSS Standards SS.2.C.1.1: Explain why people form governments. **SS.2.C.1.2:** Explain the consequences of an absence of rules and laws.

"Rules in a community are called laws," said Mrs. Miller. "Laws are created by our **government**. A government is all of the people who run a community, state, or country. Our government writes laws to keep order and to keep citizens safe. Without laws, people could get hurt."

THINK · PAIR · SHARE
What could happen if we did not have laws in our community?

Read the laws that go with each picture. Write a caption for each that tells why the law is important.

Wear a seatbelt in a moving car.

"Our government also provides many services, said Mrs. Miller. " Police and fire protection are government services. Other services include health programs and schools. People form governments to make life better for citizens."

Circle the sentences that tell why people form governments.

Keep your dog on a leash.

Cross the street at the crosswalk.

Our Constitution

"Our country's first leaders worked hard to plan a good government," said Mrs. Miller. They wanted a fair government that would keep people safe and free. Our leaders met together to write a plan called the **Constitution**. The Constitution is a plan for our government. It is a set of written laws that all Americans must follow.

NGSS Standards **SS.2.C.1.1:** Explain why people form governments. **SS.2.C.3.1:** Identify the Constitution as the document which establishes the structure, function, powers, and limits of the American government. **SS.2.C.3.2:** Recognize symbols, individuals, events, and documents that represent the United States.

"The Constitution is an important American document," said Mrs. Miller. "It protects the rights of United States citizens. The Constitution also sets up the **structure, function**, powers, and limits of the American government. This tells us how the government is organized and what each part is responsible for. It also tells us how the government should work and what it can and cannot do."

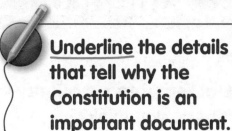

Underline the details that tell why the Constitution is an important document.

NGSS Standards SS.2.C.1.1: Explain why people form governments. **SS.2.C.3.1:** Identify the Constitution as the document which establishes the structure, function, powers, and limits of the American government. **SS.2.C.3.2:** Recognize symbols, individuals, events, and documents that represent the United States.

Lesson 4

? Essential Question How do people get along?

_____

_____

_____

Go back to *Show As You Go!* on pages 88–89. 〈〈〈

networks There's More Online!
● Games ● Assessment

5 American Symbols

? Essential Question

What represents a country?
What do you think?

_____

_____

_____

_____

Word Hunt

Find and (circle) this word:

symbol   *represent

Find 2 more new words.

_____

_____

NGSS Standards SS.2.C.3.2: Recognize symbols, individuals, events, and documents that represent the United States.

White House
The White House is where the President works and lives.

Lincoln Memorial

Symbols of Our Government

The next day, Mrs. Miller taught the students about **symbols** of the United States. A symbol is something that stands for something else. The class read about people and special buildings in Washington, D.C., that **represent** our government.

Washington Monument
The Washington Monument reminds people that George Washington was a great American leader.

NGSS Standards SS.2.C.3.2: Recognize symbols, individuals, events, and documents that represent the United States.

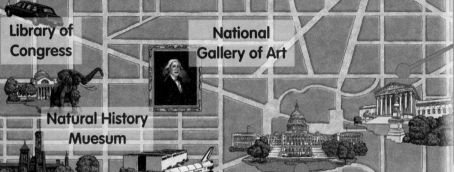

Library of Congress

National Gallery of Art

Natural History Muesum

Smithsonian Castle

Air and Space Museum

Supreme Court

The Supreme Court is where judges make sure our laws agree with the Constitution of the United States.

Reading Skill

Know and Use Text Features Certain text features can help you locate information quickly.

1. Circle the captions on the page.

2. Why are the captions helpful?

_____

_____

3. Why is the Washington Monument an important American symbol?

_____

Capitol

The Capitol is where people in our government write laws.

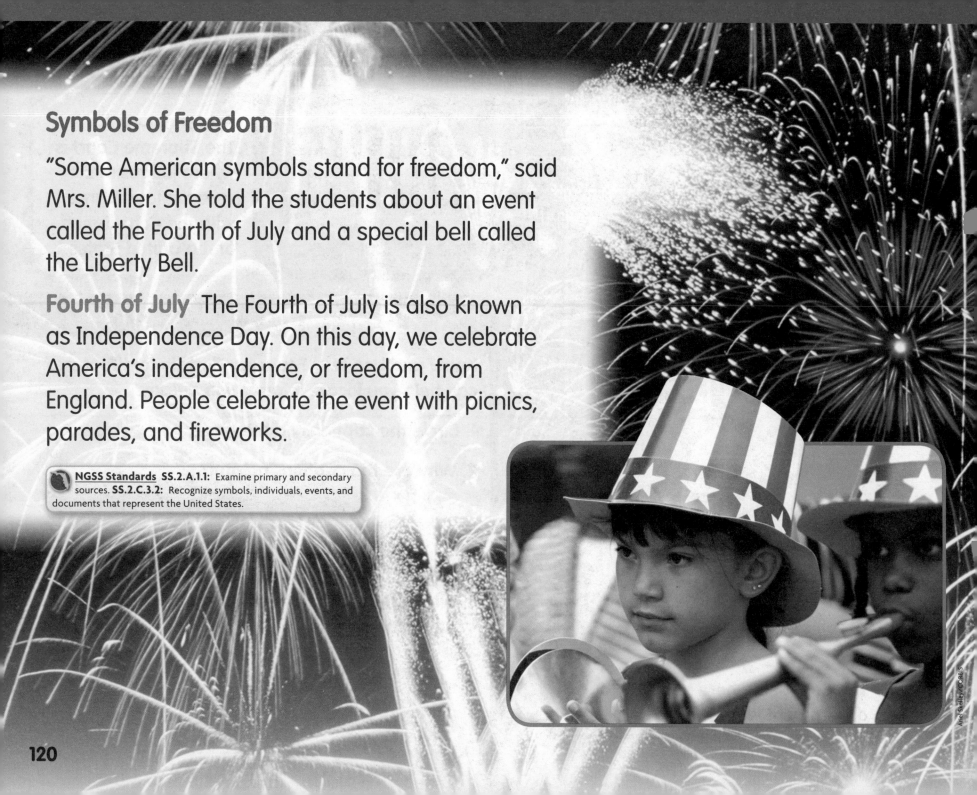

Symbols of Freedom

"Some American symbols stand for freedom," said Mrs. Miller. She told the students about an event called the Fourth of July and a special bell called the Liberty Bell.

Fourth of July The Fourth of July is also known as Independence Day. On this day, we celebrate America's independence, or freedom, from England. People celebrate the event with picnics, parades, and fireworks.

NGSS Standards **SS.2.A.1.1:** Examine primary and secondary sources. **SS.2.C.3.2:** Recognize symbols, individuals, events, and documents that represent the United States.

Ariel Skelley/CORBIS

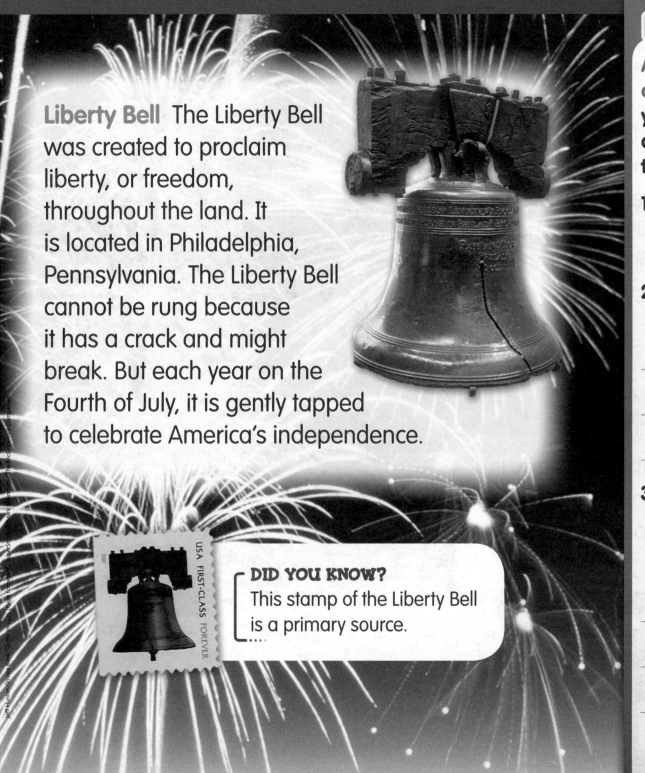

Liberty Bell The Liberty Bell was created to proclaim liberty, or freedom, throughout the land. It is located in Philadelphia, Pennsylvania. The Liberty Bell cannot be rung because it has a crack and might break. But each year on the Fourth of July, it is gently tapped to celebrate America's independence.

DID YOU KNOW?
This stamp of the Liberty Bell is a primary source.

USA FIRST-CLASS FOREVER

Ask and Answer Questions about Key Details One thing you should do when you read is ask and answer questions about the text.

1. **What do Americans celebrate on the Fourth of July?** Circle the sentence in the text.

2. **What does the word *liberty* mean?**

_____

_____

_____

3. **Write your own question about a symbol of the United States. Have a friend answer it.**

_____

_____

_____

_____

121

Symbols of Hope

"The Statue of Liberty and Ellis Island are also symbols of the United States," said Mrs. Miller. The students remembered that the Statue of Liberty and Ellis Island had special meanings for immigrants. The class read about these special symbols.

Statue of Liberty The Statue of Liberty is located in New York Harbor. It is a symbol of hope and freedom for people around the world.

NGSS Standard SS.2.C.3.2: Recognize symbols, individuals, events, and documents that represent the United States.

Lee Nelson

Ellis Island Today people visit the museum on Ellis Island to see the place where many immigrants stopped before beginning their lives in America.

Mrs. Miller asked the students to draw their own symbol of the United States. "Your symbol should show something you learned about citizens and government," she told them.

The students thought about what they had learned. Carlos chose to make a symbol about our guaranteed rights. Lena chose to make a symbol about our government. Each student began to work on their own special symbols.

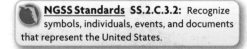

NGSS Standards SS.2.C.3.2: Recognize symbols, individuals, events, and documents that represent the United States.

Draw your own special symbol of the United States.

Lesson 5

(?) Essential Question **What represents a country?**

_____

_____

_____

Go back to *Show As You Go!* on pages 88–89.

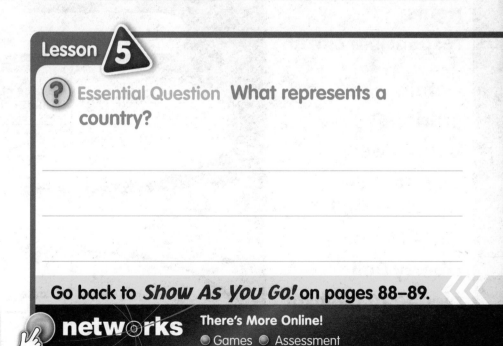

networks **There's More Online!**
● Games ● Assessment

123

4 Wrap Up

Read the details in each circle. Choose a title from the Word Bank that goes with each circle. Then choose a detail to complete each circle.

Word Bank

Titles:

Constitution

symbols

government

naturalization

rights

responsible citizen

Details:

patriotic

guaranteed

plan for our
    government

writes laws

Liberty Bell

pledge to be loyal

Title: _____

makes life better for citizens	provides services
keeps order	_____

Title: _____

Freedom of Speech	Freedom of Religion
Right to Vote	_____

Title: _____

Constitution	Statue of Liberty
Fourth of July	_____

Title: _____

self-reliant	volunteers
recycles	_____

Title: _____

sign a paper	take classes
take a test	_____

Title: _____

protects our rights	tells how the government should be run
limits the power of our government	_____

Big Idea Project

Make a mobile to show what you learned about American citizens and government.

As you work, check off each task as you complete it.

My mobile...

Yes it does!

1. explains the rights and responsibilities of United States citizens. ⬤

2. tells about the contributions of a special American. ⬤

3. tells why the government and the Constitution are important. ⬤

4. tells about a symbol of the United States. ⬤

Think About the Big Idea

BIG IDEA How do people's actions affect others? Explain the Big Idea in your own words on the lines below.

_____

_____

BIG IDEA Relationships affect choices.

Where would you go to buy food? If you said the grocery store, you are right! Food and the grocery store are related to each other. In this beginning economics unit, you will learn about how relationships like this affect the choices we make.

Show As You Go!

After you read each lesson, complete the activities to practice what you are learning!

Lesson **1**

After you read the lesson:

◯ Draw consumers shopping for goods in the grocery store below.

◯ Write a caption to explain how the grocery store meets consumers' needs.

GROCERY STORE

Lesson 2

After you read the lesson:

○ Circle the toy made in China.

○ Write a caption about trade.

Lesson 3

After you read the lesson:

○ List a personal benefit and cost of spending.

_____

_____

○ List a personal benefit and cost of saving.

_____

_____

○ What do you think the consumer below will do? Write a caption.

127

Reading Skill

Common Core Standards
RI.3: Describe the connection between a series of historical events, scientific ideas or concepts, or steps in technical procedures in a text.

Cause and Effect

Think about a time you went to the grocery store or visited the doctor. You had a reason for going. A cause, or reason, is why something happens. An effect is what happens. Thinking about causes and effects as you read will help you understand events that happen in a story.

To find a cause and effect:

1. **Read the story.**

2. **Ask, "What happened?" This is the effect.**

3. **Then ask, "Why did it happen?" This is the cause.**

Sam woke up with a cough and sore throat. He had a high fever so his mother called the doctor. As a result, the doctor said to bring Sam into the office for a checkup right away.

This sentence is the cause.

The words *so* and *as a result* link causes and effects.

This sentence is the effect.

List the causes and effects from the story in the chart below.

Cause

Effect

Read the story below. Circle the causes. Underline the effects.

Shelby and her mother wanted to make an apple pie. They needed apples, so they went to the grocery store. But the store was out of apples. As a result, Shelby and her mother chose to make a peach pie instead!

ORANGES

APPLES

.99/

2.09/

Words to Know

 Common Core Standards
RI.4: Determine the meaning of words and phrases in a text relevant to a grade 2 topic or subject area.

The list below shows some important words you will learn in this unit. Their definitions can be found on the next page. Read the words.

consumer p. 136

consumer demand p. 137

limited resource p. 138

trade p. 141

benefit p. 145

cost p. 145

FOLDABLES®

The Foldable on the next page will help you learn these important words. Follow the steps below to make your Foldable.

Step 1 Cut along the dotted blue lines.

Step 2 Fold along the dotted orange lines.

Step 3 Trace the words and read their definitions.

Step 4 Complete the activities.

Draw a picture of a consumer at the toy store.

Why is there always consumer demand for food?

____

____

Which picture shows a limited resource? Circle your answer.

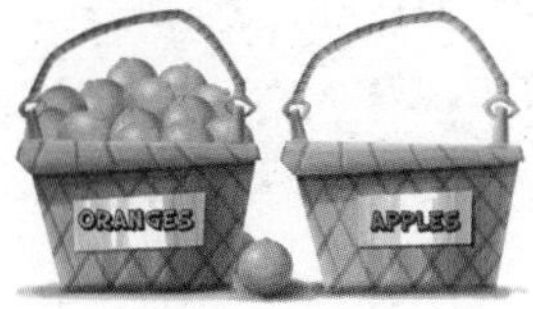

Cut Here

Fold Here

A **consumer** is a person who buys goods or uses services.

Consumer demand is the number of people who want goods and services.

A **limited resource** is a good that is scarce, or in short supply.

Do not fold

Trade means to give something and then to get something back.

A **benefit** is something good or helpful a person gets.

A **cost** is what a person gives up.

Fold Here

Write about a time when you traded something with someone.

____

____

What is a benefit of spending your money on ice cream?

____

____

Sam will save his money instead of spending it at the water park. Draw an X on the cost of his choice.

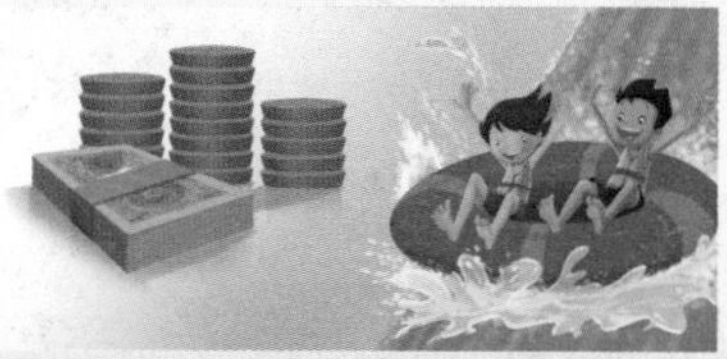

Cut Here

trade

benefit

cost

Fold Here

consumer

consumer demand

limited resource

Primary Sources

NGSS Standards

SS.2.A.1.1: Examine primary and secondary sources.

Newspapers are a type of primary source. Newspapers can help us learn about what life was like in the past. This grocery ad is from a newspaper that was printed in 1950. That is more than 60 years ago!

 Document-Based Questions

1. **Look at the ad on the right. How much money did three tall cans of milk cost in 1950?**

   _____

   _____

2. **What does this grocery ad tell us about life in 1950?**

   _____

   _____

networks

There's More Online!
- Skill Builders
- Resource Library

Meeting People's Needs

? Essential Question

How do people meet their needs?
What do you think?

_____

_____

_____

_____

_____

Word Hunt

Find and (circle) these words.

*community

consumer

consumer demand

limited resource

NGSS Standards SS.2.E.1.2: Recognize that people supply goods and services based on consumer demand.

Goods and Services

It was moving day for Sam and Shelby's family. They were moving from Grand Rapids, Michigan, to Tampa, Florida. Their new house was finally ready! Sam and Shelby were excited to be moving to their new home.

Sam and Shelby's family will need many things in their new **community**. They will buy goods and services to meet their needs. Goods are things that people grow or make to sell. Food and clothing are goods. Services are jobs that are done to help others. Doctors, teachers, and builders provide services.

Draw or paste pictures of goods in the space below.

What are two other kinds of service jobs?

**NGSS Standards SS.2.E.1.2:** Recognize that people supply goods and services based on consumer demand.

135

Doctor's Office

Book Shop

Toy Store

NGSS Standards SS.2.E.1.2: Recognize that people supply goods and services based on consumer demand.

Consumer Demand

The next day, Sam and Shelby went to their new doctor for a checkup. Then they went shopping for the things they needed. Sam, Shelby, and their parents are **consumers**. Consumers are people who buy goods and services.

Reading Skill
Use Visuals **Study the picture above. <u>Underline</u> the sentence on page 137 that tells what the consumers in the picture are doing.**

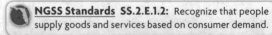

136

Grocery Store

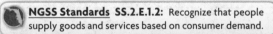
NGSS Standards SS.2.E.1.2: Recognize that people supply goods and services based on consumer demand.

There are many consumers in a community. **Consumer demand** is the number of people who need goods and services. Consumers need things like food, health care, and housing. They will buy these goods and services from people and businesses in the community.

Circle the consumers in the picture. Draw a box around the people and places that supply goods or services.

1. How do doctors meet consumers' needs?

_____

_____

2. How do grocery stores meet consumers' needs?

_____

_____

3. How do builders meet consumers' needs?

_____

THINK · PAIR · SHARE
Who supplies goods and services in your community?

137

Limited Resources

Shelby and her mother went to the grocery store to buy apples to make apple pie. But the bin for apples was almost empty. The few apples that were left also cost more money than the other fruits.

When there is not enough of a good, we say that it is a **limited resource**. A limited resource is a good that is scarce, or in short supply.

NGSS Standards SS.2.E.1.1: Recognize that people make choices because of limited resources.

DAIRY

ORANGES

APPLES

.99 /lb

2.09 /lb

138

People have to make choices because of limited resources. They may choose to pay more money for a limited resource, or they may shop somewhere else. They may decide to buy something different or nothing at all.

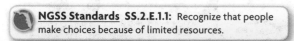
NGSS Standards SS.2.E.1.1: Recognize that people make choices because of limited resources.

Ask and Answer Questions about Key Details
When you read you should ask and answer questions about the text. Use the details from the story to answer the question below.

What can Shelby's mother choose to do since the apples are a limited resource?

_____

_____

_____

Lesson **1**

 **Essential Question** **How do people meet their needs?**

_____

_____

Go back to *Show As You Go!* on pages 126–127.

 **There's More Online!**
● Games ● Assessments

Nations Trade

How do nations work together?

What do you think?

_____

_____

_____

_____

Word Hunt

Find and circle these words.

*nation   trade

Find 2 more new words:

_____

_____

NGSS Standards SS.2.E.1.3: Recognize that the United States trades with other nations to exchange goods and services.

Trading Goods and Services

Later that day, Shelby went to the toy store to get a gift for her friend. She found the perfect gift! It was a toy manatee. Shelby noticed that the tag said, *Made in China.* "This manatee has come a long way!" she thought. Shelby wondered why the toy was made in another **nation**.

The United States **trades** goods and services with other nations to get the things people need and want. Trade means to give something and then get something in return. For example, the United States sells soybeans to China. China sells clothing to the United States. The United States trades with China.

What goods do you use that come from other nations?

_____

_____

_____

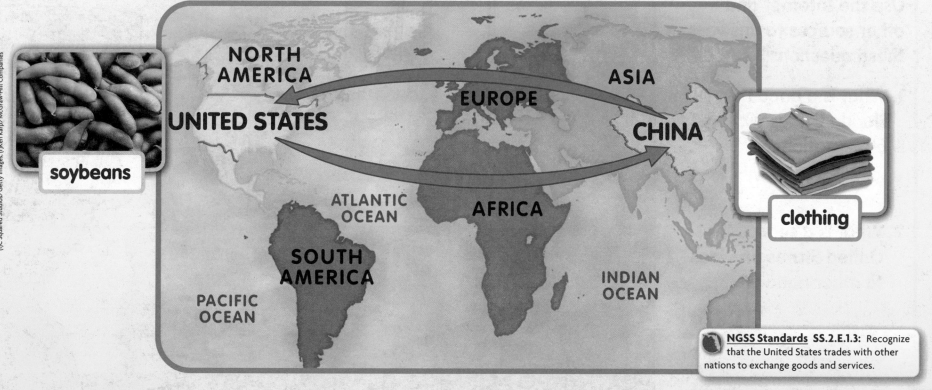

soybeans

NORTH AMERICA

ASIA

EUROPE

UNITED STATES

CHINA

clothing

ATLANTIC OCEAN

AFRICA

SOUTH AMERICA

INDIAN OCEAN

PACIFIC OCEAN

NGSS Standards SS.2.E.1.3: Recognize that the United States trades with other nations to exchange goods and services.

Trading Partners

At each store she visited, Shelby checked the goods to see where they were made. Some of the tags she saw said, *Made in Canada* or *Made in Mexico*. "I wonder what goods the United States trades with other nations," she thought. When Shelby got home that night, she used the computer to find out.

NGSS Standards **SS.2.A.1.2:** Utilize the media center, technology, or other informational sources to locate information that provides answers to questions about a historical topic. **SS.2.E.1.3:** Recognize that the United States trades with other nations to exchange goods and services.

Media Center

Use the Internet and other sources to answer these questions:

1. What is a good that Florida trades with other nations?

2. What is a service the United States provides to other nations?

142

The United States trades with nations all over the world. The chart to the right shows the top trading partners of the United States in 2010 and the goods each nation traded.

What did Shelby find out about trade?

_____

_____

_____

_____

_____

_____

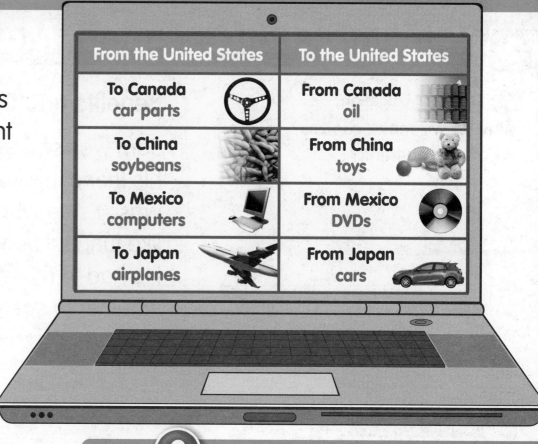

From the United States	To the United States
To Canada car parts	**From Canada** oil
To China soybeans	**From China** toys
To Mexico computers	**From Mexico** DVDs
To Japan airplanes	**From Japan** cars

Lesson 2

? Essential Question How do nations work together?

_____

_____

Go back to *Show As You Go!* on pages 126–127. ◄◄◄

There's More Online!
● Games ● Assessment

DID YOU KNOW?
Florida's top four trading partners in 2009 were Brazil, Colombia, China, and Venezuela.

Making Choices About Money

? **Essential Question**

Why do we make choices?

What do you think?

_____

_____

_____

_____

Word Hunt

Find and (circle) these words.

*choice   benefit

cost   *personal

Find 2 more new words:

_____

_____

NGSS Standards SS.2.E.1.4: Explain the personal benefits and costs involved in saving and spending.

Benefits and Costs of Spending

Sam was saving his money for a scooter. When his friend invited him to go to the water park, he wasn't sure what to do. The water park sounded like fun, but Sam really wanted a scooter!
He had to make a **choice**. He had to choose whether to spend or save his money.

When people spend money, they use it to buy something. Spending money has **benefits** and **costs**. A benefit is something good or helpful a person gets. A cost is what a person gives up. Read about the **personal** benefits and costs of spending in the chart below.

NGSS Standards SS.2.E.1.4: Explain the personal benefits and costs involved in saving and spending.

PERSONAL BENEFITS OF SPENDING MONEY	PERSONAL COSTS OF SPENDING MONEY
• You get the things you need and want now. • You get joy from buying something you wanted.	• You give up your money to get a good or service. • You give up the chance to spend your money on something else.

If Sam chooses to spend his money at the water park, what is a benefit and a cost of his choice?

BENEFIT

COST

Reading Skill

Ask and Answer Questions about Key Details One thing you should do when you read is ask and answer questions about the text.

1. Underline the sentence in the story that tells what Sam is trying to decide.

2. What was a benefit and a cost of a time you spent money to buy something?

145

Benefits and Costs of Saving

Like spending, saving money also has benefits and costs. Read about the personal benefits and costs of saving in the chart on the next page. Then help Sam decide whether to keep saving his money for a scooter or spend it at the water park.

THINK · PAIR · SHARE
What do you think Sam should do? Why?

NGSS Standards SS.2.E.1.4: Explain the personal benefits and costs involved in saving and spending.

PERSONAL BENEFITS OF SAVING MONEY

- You have more money for something you need and want.

- Saving helps you plan for the future.

PERSONAL COSTS OF SAVING MONEY

- You give up spending your money now.

- You have to wait until later to enjoy the benefit of a good or service.

If Sam chooses to keep saving his money, what is a benefit and a cost of his choice?

BENEFIT

_____

_____

COST

_____

_____

Think about a time when you saved your money to buy something. What was a benefit of your choice to save? What was a cost?

_____

_____

_____

_____

_____

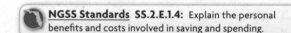

NGSS Standards SS.2.E.1.4: Explain the personal benefits and costs involved in saving and spending.

Lesson 3

(?) Essential Question Why do we make choices?

_____

_____

_____

Go back to _Show As You Go!_ on pages 126–127.

There's More Online!
- Games - Assessment

Use words from the Word Bank to complete each sentence.

Word Bank

- benefits
- choice
- consumer
- costs
- goods
- limited resource
- trades

This _____ is buying _____ at the grocery store.

The United States _____ goods and services with other nations.

The apples are a _____.
The consumer will have to make a
_____.

This consumer is thinking about the
_____ and _____ of
spending or saving his money.

Big Idea Project

Make a picture book to show what you learned. Read the list below to see what you should include in your book.

As you work, check off each task as you complete it.

My picture book...   **Yes it does!**

1. shows people who supply goods and services to meet consumer demand. ○

2. tells why people make choices because of limited resources. ○

3. tells about trade between the United States and other nations. ○

4. tells about the personal costs and benefits of spending and saving. ○

Think About the Big Idea

BIG IDEA How do relationships affect choices? Explain the Big Idea in your own words on the lines below.

_____

_____

Picture Glossary

B

*belief   A **belief** is what someone believes to be true. (page 34)

benefit   A **benefit** is something good or helpful a person gets . (page 145)

*blend   To **blend** means to mix together completely. (page 80)

C

*choice   A **choice** is when a person picks one thing over another. (page 144)

citizen   A **citizen** is a person who belongs to a country. (page 96)

colonist   A **colonist** is a person who travels to a new land to settle it. (page 69)

colony   A **colony** is a place that is ruled by another country. (page 68)

*community   A **community** is a place where people live, work, and play. (page 135)

compass rose   A **compass rose** shows the four cardinal directions and the four intermediate directions. (page 13)

Constitution   The **Constitution** is a plan for our government. (page 116)

consumer   A **consumer** is a person who buys goods and uses services. (page 136)

consumer demand   **Consumer demand** is the number of people who need goods and services. (page 137)

contribution   A **contribution** is the act of giving or doing something. (page 81)

cost   A **cost** is what a person gives up. (page 145)

crops   **Crops** are plants people grow for food or other uses. (page 41)

culture   **Culture** is the way a group of people live. It is made up of a group's special food, music, and art. (page 34)

(tc)Ryan Pierse/Stone/Getty Images, (c)Photolink/Getty Images

custom   A **custom** is a special way of doing something that is shared by many people. (page 81)

D

desert   A **desert** is a large area of very dry land. (page 47)

E

*element   An **element** is one part of something. (page 12)

Ellis Island   **Ellis Island** was an important immigration center in the United States. (page 77)

*equal   **Equal** means that something is the same as something else. (page 108)

Equator   The **Equator** is an imaginary line around the middle of Earth. (page 20)

Equator

*escape   To **escape** means to get free or run away from danger. (page 75)

F

*force   To **force** means to cause someone to do something against their wishes. (page 56)

*function   A **function** is a use or purpose. (page 117)

G

*gather   To **gather** means to collect. (page 41)

globe   A **globe** is a round model of the Earth. (page 22)

(b)The Granger Collection, NY

government   A **government** is all of
the people who run a community, state,
or country. (page 114)

H

*herd   A **herd** is a group of animals that live or
travel together. (page 44)

I

*imaginary   **Imaginary** means not real. (page 20)

immigrant   An **immigrant** is a person who leaves one
country to live in another. (page 54)

intermediate directions   The **intermediate directions**
are the directions in between the cardinal directions.
They are northeast, northwest, southeast, and
southwest. (page 13)

(t)Edmond Van Hoorick/Getty Images

*introduce   To **introduce** means to present formally. (page 96)

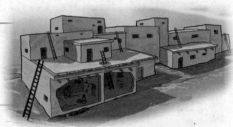

*level   A **level** is a floor of a building. (page 48)

limited resource   A **limited resource** is a good that is scarce, or in short supply. (page 138)

map key   A **map key**, or map legend, tells what the pictures on a map mean. (page 13)

map scale   A **map scale** shows how far apart places really are on a map. (page 12)

*material   A **material** is a thing needed to make something. (page 51)

N

*nation   A **nation** is a particular land where people live. (page 140)

naturalization   **Naturalization** is when a person becomes a citizen of another country. (page 96)

natural resource   **Natural resources** are materials found in nature that people use. (page 51)

North Pole   The very top of the Earth is called the **North Pole**. (page 22)

North Pole

P

*personal **Personal** means relating to a particular person. (page 145)

physical map A **physical map** shows different land and water features like mountains, rivers, lakes, and oceans. (page 18)

political map A **political map** shows the borders of states, countries, and other areas. (page 14)

*positive **Positive** means good or helpful. (page 104)

prairie   A **prairie** is an area of flat land or rolling hills covered in grasses. (page 43)

Prime Meridian   The **Prime Meridian** is an imaginary line that runs from the North Pole to the South Pole. (page 21)

Prime Meridian

recycle   To **recycle** means to reuse something. (page 105)

region   A **region** is an area with common features that make it different from other areas. (page 34)

*****represent**   To **represent** means to serve as a sign or symbol for something. (page 118)

responsible **Responsible** means able to choose between right and wrong. (page 102)

right A **right** is a freedom that we have. (page 100)

*rule To **rule** means to have power or control over someone. (page 68)

S

settlement A **settlement** is a place that is newly set up as home. (page 54)

South Pole   The very bottom of the Earth is called the **South Pole**. (page 22)

South Pole

Statue of Liberty   The **Statue of Liberty** is a large statue in New York Harbor of a woman holding a torch. (page 76)

(b)John Wang/Getty Images

*structure **Structure** is the way parts are arranged. (page 117)

symbol A **symbol** is something that stands for something else. (page 118)

T

thematic map A **thematic map** tells us certain information about a place or area. (page 12)

trade To **trade** means to give something and then get something in return. (page 141)

(t)age fotostock/SuperStock

*travel   To **travel** means to go from one place to another. (page 16)

V

veteran   A **veteran** is a person who has been in the military. (page 106)

volunteer   A **volunteer** is a person who works for free to help others. (page 104)

Index

This index lists many topics you can find in your book. It tells the page numbers on which they are found. If you see the letter *m* before a page number, you will find a map on that page.

165

Index

Index